NOSTALGIC
WAKEFIELD

The publishers would like to thank the following companies for their

support in the production of this book

ESSECO UK LIMITED

William Lamb Footwear

Lamb 1887

Ridings Shopping Centre

Woodhead Investments

YPO

....

First published in Great Britain by True North Books Limited
England HX3 6SN
01422 244555
www.truenorthbooks.com

NOSTALGIC
WAKEFIELD

CONTENTS

INTRODUCTION

For all of us, memories are the currency which we use to record the changes and progress in our everyday lives and to fix our place as individuals in the greater scheme of things. This is the latest publication in our 'Memories' series of publications, covering nostalgic reflections of towns and cities throughout the UK. In this new book we will be meandering through a pictorial cross-section of life in Wakefield over the last 100 years or so, to help satisfy the longing we all get from time to time, to recall memories of a different era that now seems better or simpler.

As we get older it is often easier to take a step back, and to view events and developments with a clearer sense of prospective. Our aim has been to assist in this respect by presenting a publication relevant to the area capable of rekindling memories of days gone by in an entertaining and informative manner. Looking through the pages of this book it is interesting to reflect on exactly how much change has taken place in the area over a short period, relative to its long history. Many of these photographs are unique and will inevitably remind us of experiences and events in our lives, of our families and of those whose influence and support has touched us to a greater or lesser degree.

Defining features about nostalgia are universal and can bring back fond memories from a time gone by. Recent research shows that nostalgia can counteract loneliness, boredom and anxiety. Couples feel closer and look happier when they're sharing nostalgic memories. People generally get a 'Warm Glow' inside when relating to events and occasions in the past and enjoy reminiscences about how things used to be – even when these events sometimes have a painful side. When people speak wistfully of the past, they typically become more optimistic and inspired about the future.

We can all remember events surrounding friends and family, holidays, weddings, special occasions and nights out in Wakefield. So let your mind wander and think of the youthful days at the dance hall or courting in one of the many cinemas in the city. Be entertained as we take you on a sentimental journey through the pages of 'Nostalgic Wakefield'…. Happy Memories!

TEXT — TONY LAX, ANDREW MITCHELL, STEVE AINSWORTH, BRENDAN O'NEILL

PHOTOGRAPH RESEARCH — BRENDAN O'NEILL, TONY LAX

DESIGNER — SEAMUS MOLLOY

BUSINESS DEVELOPMENT MANAGER — PETER HOWARD

STREET SCENES

The most recent of these views of Westgate (top right) was taken in the middle of the last century, just shortly after the last war. The type of underground public conveniences, seen in the centre of the photograph, was commonplace in most larger town and city centres. This gave rise to the euphemism for going to the lavatory of 'spending a penny' as that was the coin used when operating the lock on a toilet door. The older pictures are from the first decade of the 20th century. On one of them we can see the barber's pole, reaching out at a 45° angle. This sort of sign, with its helical stripe, has its roots as far back as the Middle Ages. Usually coloured red and white, it acts as a reminder that a barber was also often deployed as a bloodletter in medieval medicine. He sometimes performed elementary dentistry, but we will respect the sensitivities of the reader and move on to the third image here! This includes sight of the Yorkshire Penny Bank. Founded in Leeds in 1859 by Edward Akroyd as the West Riding Penny Bank, its name was soon changed to the one seen here. It became the Yorkshire Bank on the occasion of its centenary. In modern times, the site became home to the Religion nightclub. Not surprisingly, using this name for such a venture did not go down well with Stephen Platten, the Bishop of Wakefield. The handsome buildings on the right are also now largely given over to the pub and club trade.

Looking along Kirkgate from outside the old Six Chimneys house, a horse drawn bus is on its way towards us. From the evidence to be seen on the roadway nearer to the camera, quite a number of other four legged friends have passed this way. At least the rhubarb triangle, of which Wakefield is a notable member, would approve of the manure that could be collected and used on local crops. The original Six Chimneys dated from 1566, as validated by the date carved both above the door and on the gable end. It was obviously home to a very wealthy Tudor family, as only one with deep pockets could afford such a fine mansion with its state of the art smoke extraction system. Boasting an interior as grand as the outside, with its fine panelling and mighty oak staircase, this must have been one of the most handsome edifices ever to grace Wakefield, never mind just Kirkgate. By the start of the last century, the house had become a pair of shops belonging to Thompson furniture and Bell's basket making. After the First World War, the building underwent a number of alterations that weakened the structure to such an extent that it collapsed on 16 May, 1941.

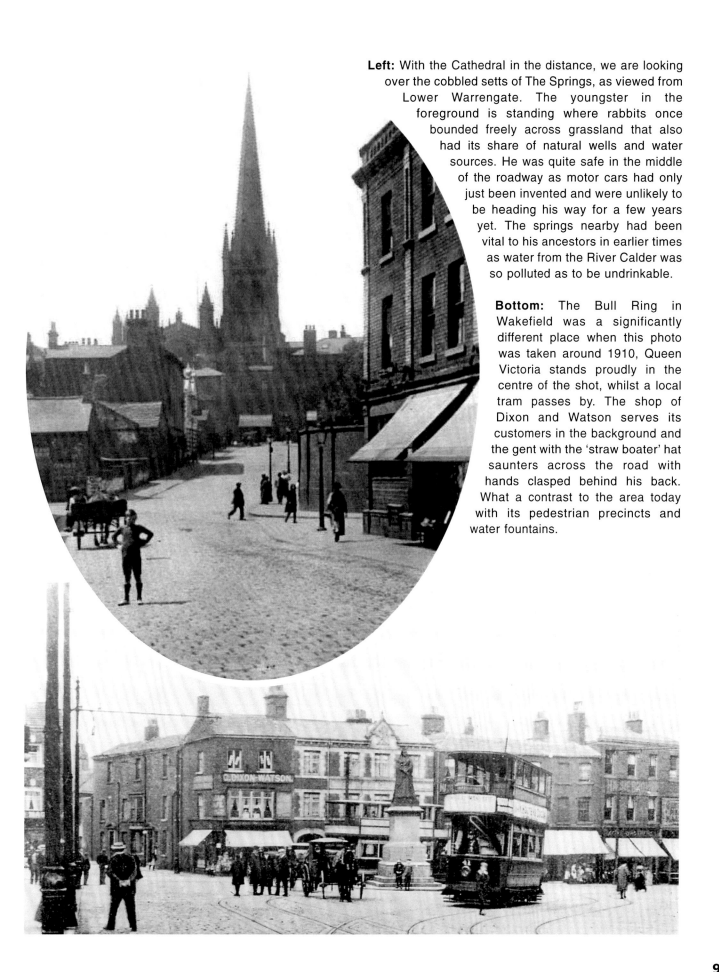

Left: With the Cathedral in the distance, we are looking over the cobbled setts of The Springs, as viewed from Lower Warrengate. The youngster in the foreground is standing where rabbits once bounded freely across grassland that also had its share of natural wells and water sources. He was quite safe in the middle of the roadway as motor cars had only just been invented and were unlikely to be heading his way for a few years yet. The springs nearby had been vital to his ancestors in earlier times as water from the River Calder was so polluted as to be undrinkable.

Bottom: The Bull Ring in Wakefield was a significantly different place when this photo was taken around 1910, Queen Victoria stands proudly in the centre of the shot, whilst a local tram passes by. The shop of Dixon and Watson serves its customers in the background and the gent with the 'straw boater' hat saunters across the road with hands clasped behind his back. What a contrast to the area today with its pedestrian precincts and water fountains.

picture we can just make out the Griffin Hotel. The bottom left picture shows the Griffin Hotel from the land that was used for the Northgate development. The pub is no more but the building, opposite the new Market Hall in Union Street, is still being used as an entertainment venue. In recent years it has been the Manor Wine Bar and Bolands Bar.

The modern view is taken from roughly from the same spot on the Bull Ring, in front of the new water feature. The roundabout has disappeared and been replaced with a paved road leading to the new buildings along Northgate. The old Griffin Hotel building cannot be seen now because of the new retail development on the right hand side. The glass building further along Union Street is Grovenor House and Jack Fultons.

These three photographs all look along Northgate and Union Street near the centre of Wakefield. The earliest image (top) shows the development of commercial units at Northgate Court, as we look across the area known as the Bull Ring. In the centre of the

t is fairly quiet in town as this Ford 100E Popular sits at the traffic lights in Cross Square. In this interesting 1962 photograph, the car and driver are waiting outside the Lotus ladies shoe shop and the well known Black Rock Inn, birthplace in the 17th century of John Potter, later Archbishop of Canterbury. On the right we can see the substantial brick built former bank premises on the corner of Wood Street and Marygate, with its unique sun dial on the outside wall. The building dates back to 1881 whn it was first occupied by local banking firm Leatham Tew & Co. Today's view across the road to Silver Street would be different with the mainly glass structure of Marygate House replacing the building in the centre of shot.

Above: Traffic was heavy in Northgate on this day in 1963, as the double-decker stops outside the Wimpy Bar. Readers who enjoy fast food will remember the early days fondly when you could get a tasty chicken sandwich 1s 6d. There is a nostalgic feel that brings back memories of the 60s and 70s. Punters with a sweet tooth could also buy jam pasties, current squares and even buttered oatcakes to go with their burger and fries. Transport was also a sign of the times with the Guy Wulfrunian in the centre of this picture. They were purchased in large numbers by West Riding between 1959 and 1965.

Below: It is not clear where this elevated photograph was taken from in July 1962, but it is approximately where the Ridings Centre Car Park is now. In the background, the tower looks like the gothic revival clock tower of the Town Hall in Wood Street, built in 1880. Beside the imposing grandeur of the Town Hall is a slightly more modern and less imposing civic offices serving various purposes, including at one time the Education Offices. This is the time of the re-development of the city centre. In the foreground where the cars are parked is the site of Chasleys Hotel, off Queen Street. Fortunately there are recognisable buildings in the Corn Exchange and the familiar pillars of the Yorkshire Bank.

Left: Is it fashion over sensibility for these two women as they walk through the flood waters in Wakefield. Although the lady coming towards us is smiling, they both probably regret coming out in ankle boots. River Calder has a history of flooding, mainly due to the high sides of its banks in its earlier stages, which cause rapid runoff of water following heavy rain. Much of the lower part of the river has been urbanised, therefore trapping flowing water within the engineered river channels. Fast flows of water cause the deposition of sediment collected from the river banks, raising the river height further. A variety of flood defences have been introduced along the Calder Valley to prevent the recurrence of floods which devastated communities in the past. In Wakefield, for example, the lake at Pugneys Country Park is used as an overflow for the river in order to protect the town.

The Bull Ring is a central point of the middle of Wakefield. It was here that a busy market was held until it moved away in 1847. A prison and the Town Hall were also located nearby. The Bull Ring probably got its name from the cruel practice of bull baiting that was seen as an entertainment in less enlightened times. Similar 'sports' in some Spanish speaking countries are still carried on under the heading of 'bullfighting'. In Britain, the bull would be tethered to a stake or hoop inside a ringed area and specially bred dogs, later known as bulldogs, would be deployed in order to immobilise the targeted animal. Bets were wagered on the length of time the poor beast would survive. This barbaric practice continued into the 19th century after an effort to ban the activity was lost in a Parliamentary vote in 1802. It was not until 1835 that the practice of bullbaiting became illegal. Seen here in the 1950s and 1960s, the Bull Ring roundabout helped change the face of this part of the city. Attitudes were altering at this time as well. The austerity of the immediate postwar decade had largely disappeared and we were in the period known as the Macmillan 'never had it so good' years, following a speech the Prime Minister made at a rally in Bedford in 1957. Further redevelopment in recent times has altered the city centre considerably once again. The spire of the Cathedral, though, remains as a constant in the distance and long may that never change.

This is a rare view of the Bull Ring from over 50 years ago, taken from the Cathedral Tower. There is no statue of Queen Victoria as she has been moved to Clarence Park, only to return in 1985. The later restructuring of the area involved the fine buildings on the left being demolished and replaced by more modern structures. On the corner of Northgate now stands Bull Ring House. The original Strafford Arms dates back to the 18th century and was Wakefield's chief posting house, with its large yard and long range of stables for the exchange of horses on the main route between London and the North. There is still a Strafford Arms pub on the site that we would regognise, but it is a modern building, the old one unfortunately demolished some years ago. Gone also is the attractive lawned area and flower beds that adorned the centre island of the Bull Ring, to be replaced with a huge water feature with 48 jets and the area is completely tiled and paved. The commercial premises still remain in Northgate Court on the right, but the store names have changed hands many times since this photograph was taken.

STRAFFORD ARMS

COOK'S

Left: A street scene that might be difficult to recognise these days, looking up Northgate. At the time of the Festival of Britain in 1951 this is how it looked. On the left by the crossing is the side aspect of the Strafford Arms hotel and further up is the Talbot and Falcon public house. This pub has a definite Irish feel today welcoming drinkers to the owners and trainers, jockeys weigh-in room at Fairyhouse Races. Further up the road are the remains of Cantor's furniture store, at one time belonging to Bleasbys. The old British cars, the Morris 8 and the Wolseley, give the photograph a nostalgic feel.

Above: By June 1970, the city was starting to feel the effects of the increase in traffic on our streets. There were more and more cars to be seen and roads began to grind to a halt in rush hour. It was time for a re-think and attention turned everywhere to improving flow in some areas and restricting access in others. The little boy crossing The Springs with his mum will be approaching middle age by now. What does he think of all the redevelopment and change to the city centre that he can recall from his childhood?

This photograph from Northgate in 1958, has a much different feel today than it does in this image. No black and white bollards and crossings anymore, infact the whole road surface has changed. If you want to cross the road you would have to wait for the traffic lights to change to red. As you swing the corner with Northgate Court on the left, the structure of the buildings remains the same but obviously the names of the businesses have changed from over 50 years ago. No more Liptons, Crooks, John Brown or Hiltons Boot and Shoe shops, more likely today to be a Pharmacy, food outlet, bookmakers or a travel shop. What also gives this picture an old look is the motor bike rider with no crash helmet, and the type of clothes being worn by the Wakefield shoppers of the time. The angled building in the distance is Grosvnor House which still stands today, but in a much more modern glass fronted form.

ENTERTAINMENT, LEISURE & PASTIMES

This page: These were the happiest days of our lives, or so previous generations would have it. You would hardly think so when looking at the grim faces of some of the students from The Girls' High School. The Spartan nature of the classroom of c1900 had little to make you smile, one supposes. It was very much a place where you did exactly as you were told and concentrated hard on the three 'r's, or else! In 1864, the Taunton Commission recommended that endowments used to further the education of boys should be extended to include secondary education for girls. In 1878, Wakefield High School for Girls was founded at Wentworth House and the doors were opened to 58 children, ranging from 8 to 17 in age. The junior section became a department in its own right three years later. Although the minds of these young ladies were developed to their maximum in academic and practical subjects, attention was also given to promoting healthy bodies. The school gymnasium boasted the best equipment that modern facilities could provide and the girls became expert in rope climbing, vaulting and beam walking. The school's former pupils include such luminaries as the sculptor Barbara Hepworth and authors Helen Fielding and Joanne Harris.

Right: The gang of young lads standing outside the fire damaged remains of the Hotel Victoria building on Finkle Street had a few years to wait before they could enter the saloon bar and sample the fine beers pulled through the pumps or take a chaser of Johnnie Walker whisky. Back in Edwardian times, the pub was largely the preserve of menfolk. The only women who frequented such places were those who did not care too much about reputations. Although coaching inns and large hotels were often smart and comfortable places, the ordinary public house was little better than a drinking den. Anyone with thoughts of being considered ladylike would avoid such a place.

1920s, the theatre had to compete against cinemas like the Picture House and in the summer live shows were replaced by films. In 1954, the theatre closed and became a picture house, and a few years later, a bingo hall. However, in 1981 it reopened as the Wakefield Theatre Royal.

Below is a great image of the Picture House, Westgate, in its pristine state not long after opening in 1913. Designed by Albert Winstanley, it was built on the instructions of Sydney Tolfree and seated 1,400 people. A mixed use venue, at one point renamed 'The Playhouse', the splendid facade has always been emblazoned with 'Picture House' across the front. It was the first of Wakefield's cinemas to be equipped for sound and "The Singing Fool" began its run here on the 8 July, 1929. By 1972, it was part of the Classic cinema chain and survived in difficult times until the mid-1980s. Subsequently, it has been used as a skateboard centre and more recently a pub and nightclub.

Two of the main entertainments venues in Wakefield can be seen in this moody photograph (above) looking down Westgate c1915. The tram is trundling up the hill past the Picture House immediately on the right, and just further down is the Theatre Royal, which dates back to 1894. Today's theatre was designed as the Wakefield Opera House, by theatre architect Frank Matcham. In the

Above: New Scarborough is a small district to the west of the city centre. These children were from Alverthorpe Road and had been enjoying the fun of the 1933 pageant. Held in June that year, this was a week-long series of civic celebrations that represented and reflected various aspects of British history. Tableaux and re-enactments showing Ancient Britons, Tudors and the Industrial Revolution were of some interest to these kiddies, but they were more taken with the processions, sports and funfair. This was the year that the new bridge over the Calder was opened, so relieving the medieval structure and its Chantry Chapel of traffic. The official ceremony was presided over by the Bishop of Wakefield, J B Seaton.

Right: Wakefield Cricket Club celebrated its centenary in 1947. This was a famous cricketing summer when Denis Compton and Bill Edrich both scored over 3,000 runs for Middlesex. Wakefield CC was originally founded as a bowling club, with the cricket section being added the following year and playing on the grounds at Grove Hall. Although the county side played a match there in 1878, the site was considered too small for the first class game. Even so, Yorkshire's Second XI regularly played here until the 1960s. The centenary celebrations included a week-long festival of sport that also included an athletics meeting. Some 30,000 attended the events. The mobile beer wagon pictured belonged to Beverley Brothers, based at the Eagle Brewery, on Harrison Street. Founded in 1861, it was taken over by Watney Mann in 1967. The cricket club folded in 1989.

Put away your mobile phones and personal music centres, children. Get out skipping ropes, hula hoops, tops and whips, chalks for hopscotch squares, marbles and conkers instead. There is so much more fun to be had and so much more imagination to be used with such toys. These could be seen in any junior school playground in the 1950s, just like the one here that might well have been Netherton Primary, Sitlington. Playtime was an occasion when children let off steam and simply had fun. Even if they had not brought any toys that day, they could still play chasing games of British Bulldog and Tig. Not only were they fun, they were free!

Above: A memory to last this young lady forever, as she is presented to the Mayor as the new Carival Queen. At this time it was quite unusual for the carnival queen to be crowned by a man, as it was tradition for a woman to do the honours. Her loyal attendants are supporting her in the background in their fabulous dresses and floral headbands. They seem to have lost a little focus and are more interested in having their photograph taken by looking straight into the camera. Maybe, several of these pretty girls have secretly harboured ambitions to wear the crown and become Carnival Queen. The carnival celebrations were an enjoyable event each summer. Long processions of adults and children in fancy dress followed the Carnival Queen and her attendants through the streets of Wakefield.

Right: The strange sight of Wakefield councillor and reigning marbles champion E E Borkwood practising in the Mayor's parlour for a "Reight Neet Aht" in 1952. The Mayor of Wakefield and nine other councillors were due to meet for the marbles cup final in a few days time. The event was in aid of local charities and the Mayor was keen to get as much practice in as possible before the big shootout. His faithful secretary, Miss Molly Taylor, is in the process of reminding him he has other civic duties as well. Unfortunately for Councillor Borkwood, his reign came to an abrupt end with the title going to his arch rival Councillor Howard, Mayor of Castleford. We wonder if the previous Mayors, pictured in the backgorund, would be looking down with a certain amount of disdain.

After King John had issued a proclamation permitting Wakefield to hold an annual fair, a further charter, this time granted by Henry III towards the end of the 13th century, gave the town additional rights. Now it was allowed to hold markets on a weekly basis and this aided the economic growth of this rapidly developing settlement. A regular market was sited in the vicinity of what became the Bull Ring. Many of the initial pitches were later converted into housing on Little Westgate, Bread Street, Butcher Row and Silver Street. Eventually, a cattle market would also be established in the town and this went on to become one of the largest of its type in the north of England. The market on Teall Street, seen not long before its closure on 16 June 1961, attracted many thousands of shoppers each year as they sought out bargains on sale in the large variety of stalls that traded here. The area was then redeveloped and an indoor replacement opened on Brook Street in 1963. This new building cost £289.000 and offered 87 stallholders a site from which to trade, along with separate fish and meat stalls. Yet another hall was opened in 2008 at a cost of £3million.

In 1935 Associated British Cinemas (ABC) opened the Regal Cinema in Kirkgate. The Art Deco building was renamed the ABC in 1962. The luxurious 1,700-seat cinema initially intoduced continuous performances - a real innovation at the time, which made it a serious rival to all other Wakefield cinemas. We can see the facade as it

looked in 1948 when the western 'Red River' starring John Wayne and Montgomery Clift was showing and later with the film 'The Iron Maiden' in 1962 when it had been renamed ABC.

We can also see the difference in the two street scenes of Kirkgate taken over ten years apart. In the main picture from 1971 the cinema in the background behind the Eastmoor Estate bus. The film showing at the time was another western, 'Monte Walsh', starring Lee Marvin. The silver screen in the living room led to declining audiences in the 1950s and 60s, but the

Regal was given a new lease of life in November 1976, when it opened as the ABC triple cinema. Sadly, despite becoming a Cannon Cinema in 1986, this too was to pass away and by the beginning of the new millennium the building stood silent and empty.

Those readers with a keen eye will spot that the bus in the foreground bears a Derbyshire registration. By the late 1960s many of Wakefield's fleet had become unreliable and 974 ARA was one of 82 vehicles purchased from other bus companies.

Within a few years of these pictures being taken, many of the families pictured on the beach would have been seduced by the promise of guaranteed sunshine and increasingly affordable package holidays to Spain. Families from West Yorkshire, like those in the photograph, would have to get used to flying abroad to blue skies and 30° heat. There would be little need for a windbreaker and everyday clothes and an umbrella would be used to keep the heat off rather than the rain. At the time these pictures were taken, you made your own entertainment if necessary. One woman may be asking the age old question, 'does my bum look big in this?'; she is perhaps conscious of causing a stir with the menfolk on the beach. Her modern, knitted two-piece swimwear was designed to catch the eye rather than for practical purposes. Those who wore knitted costumes will remember with embarrassment how heavy and saggy they got when immersed in the sea.

The first modern two-piece costume was created by Louis Reard in 1946, naming it the 'bikini' after the atoll where atomic bomb test were being carried out. Reard reasoned that the costume's effects would be akin to that of a nuclear reaction and he was not far wrong. With all the sea air and sunshine, some of the older ones took the opportunity to take a quick nap. The weather was irrelevant, what was important was getting away from work and the daily grind for a week.

Above: Beauty pageants became extremely popular with holidaymakers in the 50s and 60s and were the highlight of the summer calendar for many young women and their eager mothers. The contests were a new kind of entertainment for the growing audience of holidaymakers, as the country moved on from the greyness and austerity of the war years. In those days it was fun for all the family, the men would enjoy watching the pretty girls without getting a clip round the ear, the women would enjoy picking their favourites (or commenting on the others) and little girls would dream of being bathing beauties when they grew up. From 1958 onwards, Miss UK was a national beauty pageant held to choose a representative for the Miss World Pageant. Bathing belles from the length and breadth of Britain armed with regulation stilettos, swim suits and sash's, flocked to the next seaside event on the calendar. The lucky few went on to represent their town or city and then on to Miss UK before entering the Miss World arena, run by Eric and Julia Morley. In this photograph we can see fifteen girls in bathing costumes at Blackpool's Open Air Bath in 1967. They were taking part in the finals of Miss United Kingdom and second from the right, is Miss Wakefield Carol Richmond. The eventual winner was Miss England. Jennifer Lewis from Leicester (5th from the left), who went on to finish 4th runner-up in Miss World.

Left: "I didn't get where I am today without being able to improvise" might be what this young cheeky girl on the left would say if she was asked about this photograph now. Despite the awful weather she has still managed a smile for the camera as she makes her way along the beach. Not even the rain could dampen her fun as she used an inflatable dingy as a makeshift umbrella. At the time of this photograph in 1957, holidays abroad were still unheard and UK seaside towns provided happy holiday memories for children and adults alike.

Not a sight you see every day, as Mr Clifford Davis, of Leeds Road, Wakefield, tries out his flying machine made from bits of old pedal cycles. Following him closely down the road, are neighbours' children on 25 June, 1965. We suspect he didn't get very far, as the rotor blades look very flimsy and he has no tyres on his wheels. Nevertheless it's a bit of fun and something interesting to tell the grandchildren. It is amazing to think that this photograph was taken almost 50 years ago and the children will be approaching their 60th birthday.

WAKEFIELD TRINITY
Challenge Cup Winning Memories

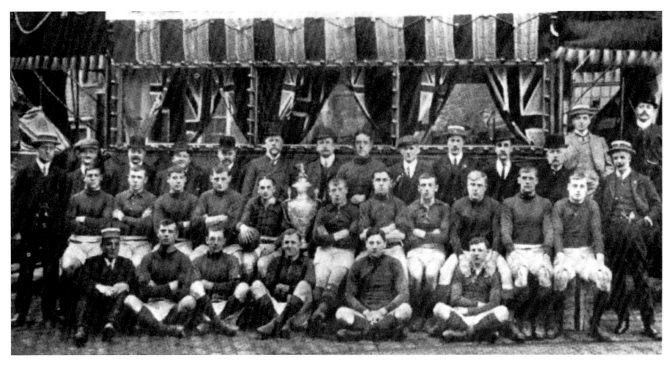

"T' Dreadnowts is comin...."

Wakefield Trinity, or Dreadnoughts, was founded by a group of young men from the Holy Trinity Church in 1873. The group played at a few different grounds before settling at Belle Vue in 1879, when the club became one of the founding members of the Northern Rugby Union in 1895.

Their status as a front runner even during these early years was evidenced when they won the Northern Union Challenge Cup for the first time in 1908/09 season, beating Hull 17-0 in the final. In the picture above, we can see the victorious squad posing for the photograph to celebrate the team's victory. The tram behind the team was decorated specially for the occasion, as well as being decorated with fairy lights for the night time journeys. The Challenge Cup Trophy is on view in the centre of shot, but rather surprisingly the captain sitting next to the trophy has a round ball resting on his leg. Despite this particular purple patch, which included wins in the Yorkshire Cup, the success lasted just a few years and, in 1914, Hull took revenge by taking the cup off the 'Dreadnoughts' in the final.

The name 'Dreadnoughts' is most likely to have come from the Royal Navy battleship of the same name, which entered service in 1906. They may have been inspired by HMS Dreadnought, which was a battleship that revolutionised naval power and was unrivalled at that time.

The first Wembley final after the war produced a return to winning ways as Trinity, with names such as Billy Stott, James "Jim" Croston, Herbert Goodfellow and Mick Exley, pipped Wigan to the Cup 13–12 and this was the start of a new and more prosperous period for the West Yorkshire side.

Pictured top right is the Beverley Brothers Brewery lorry carrying the victorious team and Challenge Cup, down Wood Street on the way to the Town Hall reception. Mass crowds had lined the streets to welcome the lads home after their heroics of having to play with virtually twelve men for most of the game. Cheering fans were taking every vantage point, including rooftops and hanging precariously out of windows, to see the procession pass by.

"The sweet smell of success"

It must have been annoying for the players as they had to put off the drinking and pass all the pubs like the Black Rock, seen in the distance, because they had a league game against Warrington the following Tuesday.

In the 1946 final at Wembley, Billy Stott of Wakefield (pictured bottom row), was the first winner of the Lance Todd Trophy introduced in the memory of New Zealand born player Lance Todd, who died in a road accident during the Second World War.

Pictured right, in January 1947, are the Wakefield and Wigan sides, when they met for the first time after the previous year's final. Both sides had an impressive array of silverware to show off. They had achieved success in their respective counties as well as being cup winners.

Top row, both teams: Baddeley, Higgins, Exley, Longley, Marson, Booth, Howes, Blan, Bratley, Atkinson, Blan, Shovaton, Ratcliff, Lawrenson, Banks, Ward, Woosey. Bottom row: Brooks, Banks, Perry, Stott, Wilkinson, Teall, Cunliffe, Mountford, Tooley and Nordgren.

"Fox and the hounds"

The club was not destined to return to Wembley again until 1960 when Wakefield emphatically beat Hull 38–5, under the guidance of coach Ken Traill and loose forward Derek "Rocky" Turner.

One of the stars of that game was Neil Fox, who can be seen above relaxing prior to his big day at Wembley. There is a definite theme of Fox and Hounds in this image of him enjoying part of his 21st birthday celebrations at the Badsworth Hunt kennels at Thorpe Audlin. Obviously Hull failed to outfox the Fox when it came to the final a few days after this event. Neil Fox went on to rack up a huge 6,220 points during his career - nineteen years of which were spent at Wakefield.

"Behind every good man is a good woman" is an appropriate saying for this photograph taken on 19 May, 1960. Wives and girlfriends of the Trinity players are joyously holding aloft the Challenge Cup after the final win against Hull a week earlier.

"Behind every good man...."

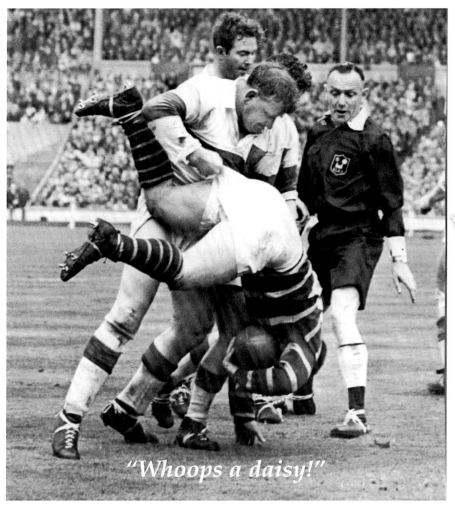

"Whoops a daisy!"

Only two years later in 1962, the lads were back at Wembley again, this time against the Fartowners. In the left photograph, Jack Wilkinson can be seen introducing himself to one of the Huddersfield forwards, with referee Mr Davies looking on. We are not sure that Great Britain forward and World Cup winner, Wilkinson, would get away with such a tackle today, but at the time he certainly made his point. He was apparently a classmate of wrestler Shirley Crabtree (Big Daddy) and it looks like he may have got a few tips from him. It was somewhat of a dour game and Trinity went on to win 12-6. Huddersfield however got their own back a few days later, as they went on to deny 'Wakey' the double in the Championship final.

The team for that day was: Round, Smith, Skene, Fox, Hirst, Poynton, Holliday, Wilkinson, Kosanovic, Firth, Briggs, Williamson and Turner (capt). In the photograph below, we can see the boys doing a lap of honour after receiving the trophy.

"A lap of honour"

The successful defence of the Cup the next year against a mighty Wigan side iced a spectacular period in the club's history with three Wembley titles in four years. Wigan were expected to win with a team of international stars including the likes of Eric Ashton and Billy Boston, but it was not the case and Trinity ran out comfortable winners 25-10, with the Lance Todd Trophy deservedly going to Wakey stand off, Harold Poynton. On the right we can see Sampson of Wakefield scoring under Wigan's posts, shortly before half time.

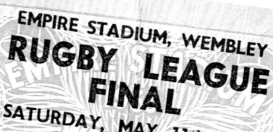

The victorious defence of the Cup in 1963 was Wakefield's fifth Challenge Cup title and part of the club's most decorated and well loved period of the 20th century.

"Between the sticks"

BUILDINGS, BRIDGES & MONUMENTS

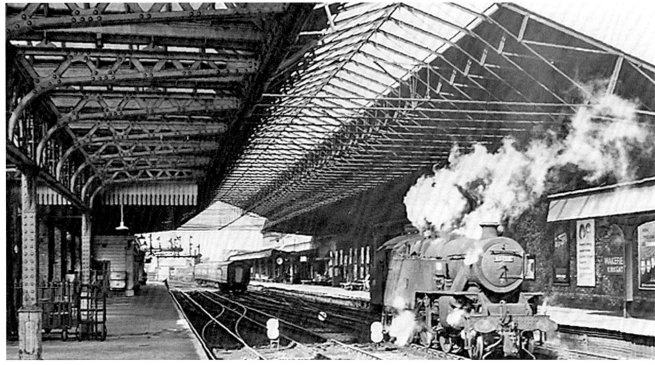

Above: Here is a photo to make all 'anoraks' purr with pleasure. The steam locomotive at Kirkgate Station was just the sort of mighty beast that traditionalists love to see on nostalgia trips run on specially dedicated lines these days. They bring back memories of time spent on platforms when we clutched exercise books and wrote down engine numbers on dog-eared pages. Scores of those records are still stored away in suburban lofts by grown men unable to let go of their childhood. But, why should they? Memories are precious and those jottings refer to an age when the world was smaller, but more memorable. Youngsters today, with their X-boxes and computer games, do not know what they are missing.

Right and top right: Wakefield is served by two railway stations. Kirkgate, seen here towards the end of the Victorian era, is unstaffed today. Over 100 years ago, it had its ticket office, porters and stationmaster. It was opened in 1840 by the Manchester and Leeds Railway Company. This building dates from 1854, but major works took place in 1972 that saw some structures on the island platform and the iron canopy roof removed. Although still operational, the station had a tired look in the earlier part of this century, but some recent refurbishment has given it a slightly fresher appearance, though it will never recapture its former glories. Most of the present services are run by Northern Rail, though some are operated by Grand Central, linking towards London King's Cross. Westgate Station, pictured top right about the time of the start of the Great War, is now our main station.

It opened in 1867 and was rebuilt in the 1960s. Some English railway stations have had parts to play in the entertainment industry. Carnforth was used in the 1945 movie 'Brief Encounter' and Widnes is supposedly where Paul Simon began composing the song 'Homeward Bound'. Westgate is featured as Denton Station in the TV series 'A Touch of Frost' that starred David Jason. The station is managed by East Coast and provides a regular and well used link with London.

More properly known as the Cathedral Church of All Saints, Wakefield Cathedral is just as impressive today as it was when photographed in the early 1900s. Since rebuilding and redevelopment it now has the tallest spire in the county. Situated on a hill in Kirkgate, it was built on the site of a former Saxon religious building, the remains of which were unearthed in 1900. A Norman church was erected here about the start of the 12th century. This was redeveloped and repaired on several occasions over subsequent years and eventually became somewhat dilapidated because of neglect. Its current glory dates from mid Victorian times when George Gilbert Scott and his son took on the significant job of its restoration. This was completed in 1874 and, after the Diocese of Wakefield was created in 1888, All Saints became its cathedral and the Reverend Walsham How its first bishop. The nave, seen here in c1940, now has a wooden roof, replacing the stone vaulted one of former times. The columns here date from the 13th century and the arches in the chancel from a century or so later.

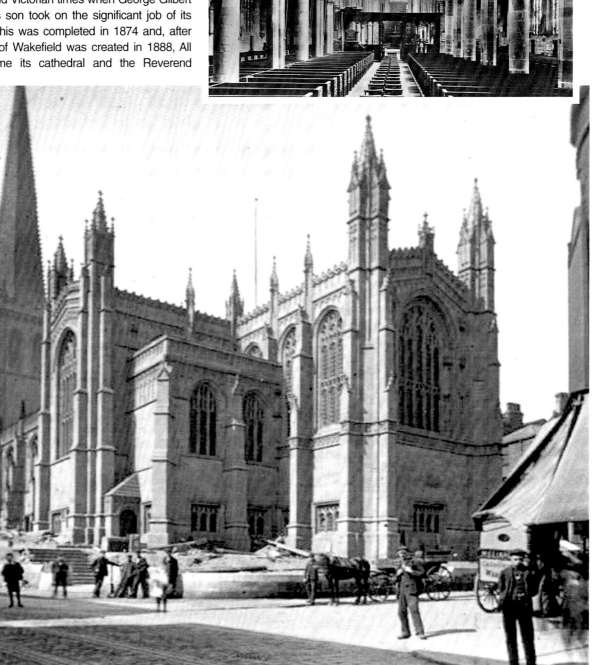

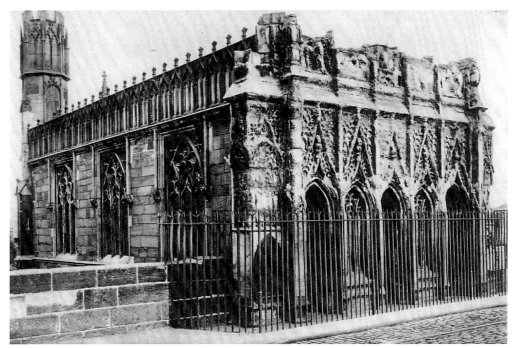

the Virgin is now a Grade I listed building. One of Britain's only three surviving bridge chapels, it dates from the mid-1300s. Original stonework can still be seen at its base, though the upper part and west front date from the late 1840s. These days it comes under the authority of the cathedral. The Chantry's original purpose was as a place where a priest could say Mass for a departed soul in order to accelerate its progress through Purgatory and into Heaven. After the Reformation in the 16th century it was used for secular purposes, including time as a cheesecake shop,

Wakefield stands on the River Calder. This waterway is crossed to the south of the city centre by the A638 road bridge. Before this opened, just over 80 years ago, traffic negotiated the medieval bridge upon which The Chantry stands. The Chapel of St Mary merchant's offices, a newsroom and for use in tailoring. The bridge was widened and strengthened in the 18th century and The Chantry was returned to church use early in the Victorian era. It remained as a chapel of ease for St Mary's until the parish was merged with St Andrew's about 50 years ago.

Right and below: A statue of Queen Victoria was erected in the Bull Ring in 1904, just three years after the death of the woman who had reigned for over 63 years during perhaps the greatest period of British history. The official unveiling, though, was delayed until 1905. Sculpted by FJ Williamson and cast by AB Burton, it was one of the former's many statues of the Queen that he designed. His creation for Wakefield was based upon one he introduced in 1887 to mark the Golden Jubilee. The memorial remained here until 1950 when it was moved to the entrance to Clarence Park on Denby Dale Road. She was on the move again in 1985 when the statue was restored to the Bull Ring. However, Victoria had not finished her travels. When redevelopment of the Bull Ring and surrounding areas got under way in the last decade, it was decided to send the old lady on her way again. In 2008, she was controversially replaced by a fountain sited in a mosaic

tiled area. The statue was winched into a new home the following year, having been cleaned and restored. It is now to be found on Castrop Rauxel Square, off Rishworth Street, looking towards County Hall.

Right: This imposing set of buildings boasts the fine architecture that makes the Mechanics Institute, Town Hall and County Hall places of which local inhabitants are justifiably proud. The Institute at the end of Wood Street is now the city's museum. It took on this status in 1955, the year in which the building celebrated the centenary of its former purpose. It had been founded as a place where adult education, particularly in technical subjects, could be offered. The building had originally been used, from its opening in 1823, as public rooms housing a music saloon, library, dispensary, newsroom, baths and bank. County Hall, on the corner of Bond Street and Cliff Parade, was built in 1898. The Town Hall that opened in 1880 was built in an attempt to rival Bradford and Leeds as the West Riding's principal centre of local government.

Below: Serenity must be the watchword for this scene. Municipal art galleries were established in growing numbers across the country in the latter years of the 19th century and into the start of the next one. However, nothing of its type was to be seen in Wakefield at this time. The Corporation acquired the Holmfield estate after the First World War and turned its grand house into a museum and art gallery in 1923. At first, there was little money around that could be used to buy works to stock the gallery. To overcome this, an art fund was established that involved Alfred Haley, a local worsted spinning mill owner. Along with others of like mind, the gallery began to be filled.

Below: This is a photograph to stir memories of old Wakefield in 1952 as we look at the junction of Cross Square and Northgate and the entrance to Bread Street. The opening of the new bus station in 1952 bought an end to the old bus office next to Teale's grocery shop. It was now obsolete and soon it was demolished. It was here you could make bus enquiries, buy your tickets, collect your parcels and recover your lost property. Wakefield was just about to undergo development and shops and businesses like Hudson's, Brown's and Teale's, despite its offer of 'Better and Cheaper', were to become part of the past in the way of new shops and new initiatives. If we stand at this corner today it is hard to visualise the way things used to be. Wakefield seemed to be in a constant process of change. Morton's faded announcement on its wall seems to reflect the mood - like the weather, bleak. Still a concern to these passers-by was rationing. It was not until July 1954 that food rationing ended, although sweets came off in February 1952; white bread came back into the shops in the previous year.

Right: The panorama across the Borough Market and Old Hall shows the view from c1951. This was a period of austerity in the land as we attempted to get back on an even keel after six years of conflict that had wrecked lives and the national economy. We owed a financial debt to the Americans that would continue to bedevil us into the next century. Although the war had ended, the world was still full of unrest. Communism was a major threat to global stability and we were in the early years of the part of history that became known as the 'cold war'. At home, rationing was still with us and people muttered that victory in 1945 had brought little in the way of home comforts as a result.

Above: Lewis Hughes of Wakefield was more than just a shop in the centre of town, for this shop could claim to be one of the longest established retailers in Wakefield. The sign above the shop, confirms it as having been in existence since 1785, setting up business in the Bull Ring as an Italian Warehouse. The mind boggles to think that Italian produce and wines were transported across Europe to Wakefield in the late 1700s, but confirms the importance and affluence of the city at that time, trading in corn, coal mining and textiles. In 1785, George III was on the throne and William Pitt, The Younger, was Prime Minister, it was also the year that the first gas balloon was flown across the English Channel. This photograph taken in the 1960s shows the signs above the windows, offering 'everything for your cocktail party', South African Sherries and the 'largest selection of wines and spirits in the city'. Sadly, this shop was demolished in the mid-1960s just after this photograph was taken.

The main photographs on these two pages show an interesting perspective to the area around Carr House Flats in the swinging 60s. They give a unique look from above of the buildings and land, across from the cathedral, that today is occupied by the Ridings Shopping Centre. The prominent Carr House Flats, with 11 floors and built out of brick, are now amazingly over 50 years old. The flats tower over Queen Street car park, which in this photograph has getting on for 100 of our favourite cars from the 60s. Perhaps this was the most iconic age of the car as it provided us with some of the most instantly recognisable vehicles. It was a time when automobiles were cool and everyone wanted to own one. Almost every car maker is included from the likes of, Ford, Vauxhall, Rover, Morris, Jaguar and Volkswagen.

In the photograph top right we can get a real retro feel about the furniture and design of the flats back in the 60s. Modern Scandinavian furniture, with teak or rosewood sideboard and obligatory wooden coffee table became a distinct style of interior design in the 1960s. Fashion was becoming more about bright colours and they were evident in the carpets, curtains and accessories

Ballroom dancing was a popular leisure activity in Wakefield in the 50s and 60s and the BBC's 'Come Dancing' brought the competition into the living room through the TV set. If you wanted to go out dancing, as may did, there was the Embassy Ballroom and in 1959, Mecca opened the Locarno on Southgate. We can see the building in this photograph from the 60s, and also in the bottom left hand corner of the main image. The name was changed to Tiffany's in 1970 and ten years later, it was closed for demolition to make way for the new Ridings Shopping Centre.

Right and facing page: It was the beginning of the end for the Grand Electric Cinema and Betty's Snack Bar in this reminder of Wakefield's past. They were housed in the great classical Corn Exchange building, designed by W. L. Moffat of Doncaster, which stood on this site until the early 1960s. The Assembly Rooms on the first floor of the handsome building were in frequent use in the Victorian period for concerts, bazaars and all manner of public meetings. Even in the middle of the 19th century, despite its mining industry, the town was best known as a centre for grain. Its Corn Exchange, built in 1838, had the reputation of being the finest building in the town, but even this did not save it from demolition. In the early twentieth century the Exchange floor became a roller-skating rink and the Assembly Rooms were converted in 1910 into the Grand Electric Cinema. Unfortunately, by the time of this photograph in 1963, the cinema industry had gone into a period of decline and cinema audiences in this country had fallen by two-thirds compared to the early 1950s. Television became the staple entertainment and 'Housey Housey' became Bingo and a national pastime. The Grand Electric was to suffer like so many others. Why pay to go to the 'Ranch', as it was nicknamed, when you could stay at home and watch westerns like 'The Lone Ranger' and 'Rawhide' in your front room for nothing?

Left: This is a very old photograph of the late 18th century Black Rock public house in Cross Square. The Grade II listed building has some history and a very interesting past. It is on the site of the house where John Potter lived as a child. He was to be Archbishop of Canterbury from January 1737 until his death in 1747. This was his family's home above his father's drapers shop. The house was converted into a public house in the early twentieth century. The front has remained virtually unchanged over the years with its centre Venetian window and a wide eliptical arch decorated in glazed tiles. It is not clear if this gentleman is Charles Henry Cutts, but if he was around today, he would have to go out the back for a smoke.

55

Above: It was a sad day when the bulldozers moved in to begin their demolition in the summer of 1962, exactly 111 years after it was built. A great many local people felt very strongly that the old market should have stayed. The demolition was a typical example of architectural purges in the 1960s, when many Victorian buildings across the UK were replaced with high-rise concrete and glass buildings. The gaily-striped canvas covers of the open market were gone for good as the workmen, in flat caps not hard hats as today, loaded the remainder of the demolished building onto the back of a wagon. Disruption, however, was minimal as they were able to carry on selling from stalls in the open market. Viewed from Westmorland Street before the main market hall was demolished, the building still retains much of its original character . The fine old building was opened on 29th August, 1851, and whether you wanted a second hand coat or a cauliflower, Wakefield market was where you would find it. Wakefield has had markets since 1204, and long before this building was constructed it had established itself as the place to find a bargain. A man once bought a wife here back in the 19th century, though history is silent on whether or not the lady turned out to be a bargain!

Right: A fabulous photograph from over 60 years ago showing a steady flow of lorries and cars on the A61 Wakefield to Barnsley road at Newmillerdam, south of Wakefield. There is an atmosphere of peace and tranquillity in this view, where water flows swiftly over the weir and under the bridge and water-loving plants grow thickly at its edge. Formerly known as Thurstonhaigh, the village got its current name from the construction of a grain mill powered by water from the dammed lake, thus the 'New mill on the dam". The present Corn Mill was rebuilt in the 19th century, though there was a corn mill here back in the 13th century - possibly as early as 1280. The mill was in use until as recently as 1960. In 1975 fire swept through the old building, gutting the interior, after which it was restored and converted into a pleasant modern restaurant. In the distance we can see Hill Road and to the left is the Grade II listed 'The Dam Inn'.

Above: Some readers may well remember the old White Swan pub on the A638 Kirkgate road, near the city centre. The railway bridge gives an indication that off to the right is Kirkgate station. It was a sign of the times at the beginning of the 60s that the main subject of advertising was either beer or cigarettes. On the left we can see a Ford Popular which would have been a brand new model at the time. Outside Hopkinson's is the Morris Minor closed van designed for commercial use with small businesses. Versions of the Minor were built from 1953 until the end of production in 1973.

EVENTS & OCCASIONS

King George V and Queen Mary paid a visit to the north of England in 1912. They were just two years into their positions as our monarch and consort. Nowadays, we are well used to seeing royals on a walkabout, but this was something of a novelty in those days when the class divide was still a significant social factor. 'Them and us' did not mix as easily as they do today. The couple set something of a trend in calling in on ordinary people at their workplaces during a tour of industrial sites, mining communities and factories. They began in South Wales, before moving on to the West Riding. On 10 July, they visited the premises of the Seamless Boat Company and Edward Green's factory that made fuel economisers for steam boilers.

They also took time to tour George Craddock's wire rope works and the King took time to sign the visitors' book there. King George's interest in communicating with the working classes stood him in good stead in later years. His cousins, ruling Russia and Germany, were either murdered or deposed by the end of the decade. By then, he was head of the House of Windsor having sensibly renamed it from Saxe-Coburg-Gotha in 1917.

The King and Queen can be seen in this photgraph leaving Bagley Brothers glass works after a visit in 1937. Bagley's was situated by the canal in Knottingley and was once the country's most successful glass manufacturer, with a reputation for fine quality that stretched well beyond our shores. In the 1930s, under the management of Stanley and Percy Bagley, a range of decorative glass with the name of 'Crystaltynt' was introduced. To mark the occasion of the Royal visit, employees were presented with a special glass plate. King George VI and Queen Elizabeth can be seen here with members of the family firm. This was Trafalgar Day, 21 October, 1937, and the Royal couple went on to a reception in their honour at the Town Hall.

Above: It was a little fanciful, but 1933 was declared to be the 'Wakefield year of progress'. This crowd of happy souls seemed to be enjoying the festivities that were part of the week-long celebrations and included a pageant that was good fun for everyone. Of course, we were in need of something to lift our spirits. This was the era of the Depression when millions were unemployed or on short time. If you could not feed the family, there was little that you could cheer about.

Left and below: It was a very special occasion for Wakefield crowds to come out in these numbers and occured when Field Marshall Montgomery was awarded the Freedom of the City in 1947. The crowds pictured here in Wood Street covered almost every inch of space available, slowing Monty's car down to a snail's pace. The procession of cars can just be made out in the middle of the crowd in the mid distance. Union Jacks and bunting are visible everywhere, with only a handfull of police on duty to control the thousands of locals in the city centre on the day...spot them if you can!

Above: Respectful crowds line the city centre streets as the formal procession passes in February 1946. The occasion is the enthroning of the Rt Rev Henry McGowan as the new Bishop of Wakefield. The procession included senior police officers, mace bearers, local dignitaries and representatives of the law, as they made there way from the Town Hall to the Cathedral. An eminent Anglican Bishop in the first half of the 20th century, Bishop McGowan was born in 1891, educated at Bristol Grammar School and St Catharine's College, Cambridge, and ordained in 1914. He was Vicar at St Mark, Birmingham, and Emmanuel, Southport, before becoming Rural Dean and then, in 1938, Archdeacon of Aston. In November 1945 he was appointed Bishop of Wakefield and consecrated in February 1946.

Right: The May Queen was being led along like some latter day Lady Godiva. Happily, she was able to retain her carnival robes and did not have to copy the 11th century noblewoman in the way she made her mark on the streets of Coventry. Our Queen was happy as she was, milking the applause and being thoroughly delighted with the reception she was getting. Somewhere in the crowd, a proud mum smiled a secret smile as she nudged a neighbour and said, 'Isn't she lovely?'

Below: Harold Wilson meets some of the miners children at the Annual Yorkshire Miners' Demonstration and Gala in Wakefield, June 1967. The pipe smoking Prime Minister seemed in good spirits in the Yorkshire sunshine as he mixed with the local crowds. It was a difficult time for the leader. After a costly battle, market pressures forced the government into devaluation. Wilson was much criticised for a broadcast in which he assured listeners that the "pound in your pocket" had not lost its value. It was widely forgotten that his next sentence had been "prices will rise". Economic performance did show some improvement after the devaluation, as economists had predicted. The devaluation, with accompanying austerity measures (we know all about that), successfully restored the balance of payments to surplus by 1969.

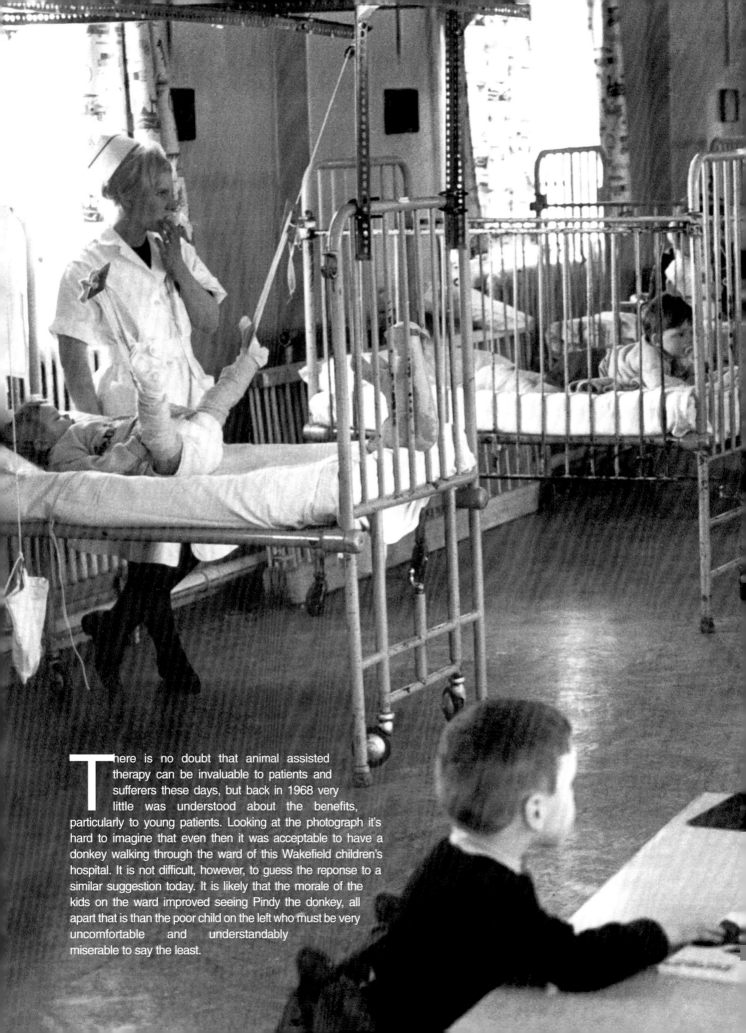

There is no doubt that animal assisted therapy can be invaluable to patients and sufferers these days, but back in 1968 very little was understood about the benefits, particularly to young patients. Looking at the photograph it's hard to imagine that even then it was acceptable to have a donkey walking through the ward of this Wakefield children's hospital. It is not difficult, however, to guess the reponse to a similar suggestion today. It is likely that the morale of the kids on the ward improved seeing Pindy the donkey, all apart that is than the poor child on the left who must be very uncomfortable and understandably miserable to say the least.

ON THE HOME FRONT

This immaculately dressed young lady was known as 'Young Kitchener' and she sported the correct military attire down to gloves, spurs and swagger stick. During World War One, 'Young Kitchener', stood on her own collecting money for comforts for the troops. Her placard read that she was collecting for soldiers' and sailors' parcels and appealed to the public to, 'Please spare a copper'. No doubt her charming appearance touched many hearts, especially those with loved ones far away and she raised an estimated £4,000, the equivalent of a staggering £390,000 in today's terms. The date on the photograph is a poignant one, for that was the very year the real Kitchener, Minister for War, launched his famous poster recruiting campaign. This was one of the most enduring images to emerge from the Home Front - Kitchener with his handlebar moustache, fierce gaze and pointing hand. 'Your Country Needs You'. Thousands answered the recruiting call, stirred by simple patriotism, many from West Yorkshire.

at war and mums having to take up the work of the men who had gone overseas to fight. The young lad in the plane looks comfortable enough whilst his friend, possibly his brother, has been well dressed in his police sergeant's uniform complete with truncheon, gas mask and helmet. A young girl looks on in admiration and may well have a costume of her own for the possible celebrations.

Below: We had it pretty tough during the last war. Our diet was heavily concentrated on what we could grow or produce for ourselves and, with food rationing in force as well, we were well used to a reliance on vegetables to fill our stomachs. But, at least the enemy had been kept at bay. Pity those people whose lands had been invaded and homes destroyed or confiscated. Things were so bad in the

Above: 'Ello, 'ello, 'ello. What have we got 'ere then? Someone has gone to a lot of trouble to put this scene together. What, with the making of the model aeroplane, the uniforms and the hats, it makes a delightful picture from the 1940s and could well have been in support of the war effort. Galas and processions gave everyone a lift during difficult times of rationing, dads being away

Netherlands that its people were reduced to eating tulip bulbs to ward off starvation as crops failed and food supplies cut off by the retreating German army. Pictured in February 1946 outside the Town Hall, this young group of 130 Dutch evacuees had spent two months in Wakefield to help them recuperate after their ordeal.

wise precaution even if the fear of a gas attack never materialised.

During the last war there were frequent salvage drives. It was a waste not, want not culture and full of suggestions about making do and mending. Raw materials were scarce and anything that could be recycled was put to use. Those of us in the 21st century who think of ourselves as being 'green', and of being among the first to counteract the throwaway society, should look back to the 1940s. Here we can see that children collected all sorts of stuff that could be turned into something useful. Anything from an old envelope to a garden rail was collected and transported to a sorting centre.

In the late 1930s, as the outbreak of war seemed a certainty, civil defence groups began organising their strategies and trained members in the use of measures that would help combat the effects of modern warfare on the civilian population. The issuing of gas masks and instruction in their use was one such measure. All schoolchildren were issued with them in the early summer of 1939 and they carried them in purpose-built boxes to and from lessons. At the start of September 1939, any youngster being evacuated from the major urban areas clutched a battered suitcase in one hand and a gas mask in the other. Babies also had special helmets into which mothers would have to pump air with a bellows. Even the police were expected to don the less than flattering apparatus, but it was a

There, armies of volunteers sifted and graded rags, bones, paper, metal and any other items that could be put to further use. Throughout the war years, appeals for junk and salvage were ongoing. Sometimes we were asked to hand over old saucepans, flat irons and bedsteads to provide scrap metal for the building of new warships and planes. It seemed ironic that the Spitfire overhead might really be a flying frying pan. Not to worry, as long as it did its job. The British, weaned on a diet of jumble sales and white elephant stalls, were past masters (and mistresses) at scavenging. The skill was to serve them well.

The role of women in two world wars cannot be underestimated. The men departed in their millions, leaving behind factories, engineering works, farms and public transport vehicles without anyone to operate them. Step forward the fair sex. They tilled the fields and chopped down trees. Women handled heavy engineering plant and served in factories geared up for the war effort. They got behind the wheel of ambulances, tractors and trams and even took on new skills, such as servicing aeroplanes for the Royal Flying Corps. Towards the end of the war, those with a particular determination put on uniforms and joined the Women's Auxiliary Army Corps or Women's Royal Air Force. It was more of the same, but on a larger scale and with greater organisation, the second time round. When the balloon went up in 1939, there were already women's organisations officially in place.

Army'. During the blackout, cries of 'Put that light out' and 'Don't you know there's a war on?' were often mimicked by comedians as part of their variety acts, but most wardens played an important role during the grim days of the early 1940s when we were under attack. They were often in the thick of it, assisting the general public find shelter during an air raid. They also reported the extent of bomb damage and assessed the local need for help from the emergency and rescue services. The wardens used their knowledge of their local areas to help find and reunite family members who had been separated during an air raid.

Stella, Lady Reading, founded her Women's Voluntary Service in 1938 and her members had already played their part in preparing the public for war on the home front with various civil defence training exercises. As men set off overseas, yet again women juggled home and family management with the demands of keeping the wheels of industry and food production turning. The Land Army was reformed in July 1939. Some 113,000 women, a third of all those employed in agricultural work, had done their bit in the service that was introduced in 1917. When peace was declared in 1945, there were 460,000 women in uniform and 6.5 million in civilian war work.

'What are you doing, mister?' The warden was using the telephone box as a handy resting spot as he filled out some return or checked a particular detail on his log of events. He was a member of the Air Raid Precautions (ARP) team of civilians who offered their services as volunteers on the home front. Many were in jobs that had a protected status as their work expertise was invaluable to wartime production. Others were too old or unfit to join up, but still wanted to play their part. There was also a small handful who just enjoyed being officious and belonged to what came to be known as the 'jobsworth' mentality. Such a type was admirably portrayed by Bill Pertwee as Warden Hodges in the BBC sitcom 'Dad's

Above: At first glance this looks like a very dangerous practice, but no need to worry. This is the Army Salvage Unit at a munitions dump in 1940. These unexploded German bombs have been emptied of explosives and are being cut up for scrap using oxy-acetylene torches, overseen by an officer. It was an ironic aspect of the war that bombs dropped by the enemy could in some cases be recycled into bombs which could then be dropped on them. Again, it was all part of the National Salvage Scheme with every possible item being recycled in support of the war effort.

Below: The war came to Wakefield on 28 August, 1940. This was in the period that everyone now calls the Blitz. All across the land, the Luftwaffe targeted centres of industry and heavy engineering vital to the war effort. In Yorkshire, Sheffield, with its steelworks and armament factories, and the docks at Hull were badly hit on many occasions. The enemy also had 'softer' victims in its sights when it bombed the homes we lived in, leaving shattered lives as well as houses in its wake. Norton Street, in Belle Vue, suffered badly when several properties were wrecked, with injuries to residents being in double figures. Industrial areas along the Calder and the canal, as well as the Sykes plant at Horbury, that had begun manufacturing goods for use in the war effort, were of interest to the bombsights of the Junkers and Heinkels overhead.

Above: Baby's bath time - not quite bath time in this scene as we see mothers and helpers washing clothes and toys in small tin baths. We can see someone's teddy bear lying on the table and the children having their hands washed. Aprons were the garment to protect every day clothes as they had to last as long as possible, given the high relative costs of replacing them.

Top right and right: It was possibly the acute wartime shortages of food and supplies which made doctors, health workers and mothers alike very aware of the health of the new generation, and children were carefully weighed, measured and immunised against illness, For many of us, it is difficult to imagine life before the NHS, when healthcare was unreliable and treatment had to be paid for. During the

war, children had their own ration books which entitled pre-school children to an allowance of cod-liver oil and orange juice. Long before the advent of the cod liver oil capsule, the recommended spoonful of cod liver oil was administered to the youngest children every day. Children might have screwed up their noses at the fishy taste, but the nourishing cod liver oil went a long way towards keeping them healthy. The vitamin-packed orange juice was far more palatable, and artful mothers would often use the orange juice as a bribe.

Later it became available as 'cod liver oil and malt', a totally acceptable brown sticky substance that tasted like toffee and had to be spooned out of a large jar. It has been said that child nutrition in the 1950s was superior to today, according to researchers - despite the food shortages of the post war period. Modern children fare worse for intake of several key nutrients, including fibre, calcium, vitamins and iron. In fact, rather surprisingly, the 1950s diet was almost in line with current recommendations on healthy eating for children.

AROUND THE SHOPS

Hague Bros and Kingswell and Son's linen drapery on Northgate are a neat link to the past glories of Wakefield and the textile industry. By the start of the 19th century, our home had become a wealthy market town thanks to a profitable trade in wool and grain. Its position as an important inland port was established by easy access to the Aire and Calder and Calder and Hebble Navigations, along with the Barnsley Canal. By the time of this photograph, taken c1930, the former influences upon the economy had begun to wane in importance. Goods were moved by rail and road and waterways had become largely redundant. The job of the traffic policeman, as we can see in the photograph, was becoming increasingly important.

Above and below: Two views of Northgate either side of the last war suggest that this was one of the quieter spots in the city. Perhaps the camera does lie after all as this has, for many years, been a busy thoroughfare, part of the A61 that heads off in the direction of Leeds. The 1951 photograph shows the junction with Providence Street, the road that today takes you infront of Woodhead House and the Co-op Bank. The older panorama shows the Cathedral in the distance. At the time it was pictured, Europe was getting ready to face its second major crisis in just two decades. The First World War was only a generation away and here we were, on the brink of another turmoil that would lay waste to vast tracts of the Continent yet again. Northgate is one of Wakefield's oldest areas. Mentioned in the Domesday Book as 'Wachfield', there was a settlement here that dated from Saxon times. Despite falling victim to the form of scorched earth policy adopted by the invaders during the Norman Conquest, Wakefield rose from the ashes and was sufficiently successful to be awarded the right to hold its own annual fair by King John in the 13th century.

Above: More than a century has passed since this Edwardian scene on Upper Kirkgate was captured. It was obviously a very busy part of the city, with shoppers and office workers mingling on the pavement and crossing over the tramlines that were also littered with horse droppings. Life in that era was one that saw great changes. The noble steed worked in harness, as it were, with new-fangled electricity and engine power. Before long, the skies above our heads would be dotted with the sort of flying machines that were being trialled in such faraway places as Kittyhawk in America.

Below: Who would have thought it? Woolworth was a name on Britain's High Streets that seemed destined to last forever. Virtually every town had an outlet belonging to the original five and ten cent store that crossed the Atlantic in 1909 when its first store opened in this country in Liverpool. By the interwar years, 'Woolies', as it was affectionately known, was everywhere. Selling cheap and cheerful merchandise, along with its pick 'n' mix confectionery and cheap cover version LPs, the chain store's popularity continued deep into the 20th century. But fierce competition from other companies saw its rapid demise. By 1997, the parent company had folded and the UK branch went the same way a decade or so later. The shop at 45 Kirkgate closed on 2 January, 2009, and became an Iceland store.

now a listed building, with Wood Street to the left and Cross Square to its right.

Below: The improvements to the Bull Ring seen here in the early 1950s, meant the removal of the statue of Queen Victoria and the provision of an open space of flower beds and grassed surrounds. This roundabout with its 'Keep Left' signs, adequate at the time, gave useful information as to how to approach it. It looks as though there may be a coming together as the Land Rover pulls out of Northgate into the path of the classic 1940s saloon car. It could be a Triumph Twelve or Sunbeam Talbot Ten, or similar. Lets hope it ended well. After the end of the Second World War when petrol became available for leisure use - albeit still on ration - cars started to trickle back onto British roads. We can see here the beginnings of the trend of the domination of town centres by non-local shops. What is local here, however, is the Beverley Brothers Brewery, famous for its 'Golden Eagle' ale from the Eagle Brewery in Harrison Street but not for long, unfortunately. By the 1960s it had suffered the fate of many a local brewery.

Above: The Grand Clothing Hall was designed by Percy Robinson and opened in 1906 as an imposing presence on the Bull Ring. Its delightful Italian Renaissance style of architecture acts as a slap in the face for those of a brutalist persuasion who built concrete, steel and glass monstrosities in the 60s and 70s. It was a much-loved outfitters for many years, reflecting the importance of wool and other textiles in the historical economy of Wakefield. It prospered as a hub for trade in both raw materials and finished goods. As business declined in Victorian times, we moved on to focus upon worsted spinning. The Hall later became home to a number of varied retail outlets and is

Above and below: The George Hotel formerly occupied this large area next to British Home Stores, in Kirkgate, pictured in 1955. New shops for Brown Brothers & Taylor would be built here to provide a more modern approach and as much needed uplift to this area of the city. The elevated view shows the parade of shops on Upper Kirkgate in the autumn of 1956. You would have thought we had had enough of global conflict after the Second World War, but that had only finished a little over a decade earlier and now we were involved in more problems overseas in what became known as the Suez crisis. About the same time, Hungary was being overrun by tanks belonging to the Soviet Union and Israeli forces crossed the Egyptian border and entered the Sinai peninsula. The Cold War was hotting up, it seemed.

Above: This nostalgic image from the late 50s or early 60s, shows the upper part of Westgate. Just along from Clydesdale's electrical and furniture store, which is receiving a delivery, is the Corn Exchange building. The grand old building on the right has served many purposes throughout the years. Wrestling, roller skating, once the Grand Electric Cinema, and as far back as 1849, it was the scene of the great Free Trade dinner. On this wet January day in 1962 there are few traffic problems despite the lack of road markings. At this time a push bike can be left safely without chains and padlock in between the two parked cars. It might be safer however for the chap crossing the road to look to his right rather that staring at the cameraman. On the left, is the rather grand A55 Cambridge Mark II, with leather trimmed front seats spaced closely together to allow a central passenger to be carried. A rather more humble Ford Popular is on the right. An interesting photograph in many ways, with perhaps the old Corn Exchange serving as reminder of what this part of Wakefield was like over 50 years ago.

A busy scene on Teall Street in July 1970, looking from the Kirkgate end up towards The Springs. The fashions of the time are out in force, with flared jeans, tank tops and the ever-present 'Mackintosh' all in view. To the left is an Austin A40, which was the forerunner to our now ubiquitous 'hatchback'. It was versatile, economic and reasonably reliable, with a boot that could be accessed from either the rear seat or the back of the car. The then, new market hall was a contrast to the old buildings of Wakefield and was completed in 1964. There would, however, be much more modernisation to come for the centre of Wakefield, with the streets in the photograph becoming totally pedestriansied in later years. It is certain that in today's Wakefield, private cars would not be able to park directly outside the shops, but that does make it all the nicer for the shopper who likes to stroll around the centre of this lovely city.

Right: As the two ladies cross Kirkgate in May 1964, chatting away, a van on the opposite side of the road has parked up outside the Double Six public house. The photograph was taken just prior to a period of extensive change in Wakefield. It would be only a few years later before the majority of these buildings had disappeared for good, at the hands of the demolition men. We can see some of Wakefield shoppers' favourite haunts, including, Cavendish furniture shop and Hiltons boot and shoe shop. If you wanted to go for a swift drink before getting the bus home, you could call in the Double Six or, slightly further along, the 'Criterion'. We can easily recognise the John

Smith's Magnet Ales sign on the wall outside. Brewing was big business, and by 1967 John Smith's was the third largest regional brewer in the country after Courage and Scottish & Newcastle breweries. The vehicles in this picture add to the nostalgic feeling and one never to be repeated.

Below: From art deco to Yorkshire stone to concrete and brick, this scene along Upper Kirkgate has them all. The shop fronts of Stimpsons, Dunn & Co., Greenwoods and Dolcis can be seen. Just take a look at the lady in the centre of the photograph who is proudly pushing her baby in the popular Silver Cross

pram between the traffic, avoiding the Austin which is making its way to the top of Kirkgate. Silver Cross was one of the leading pram makers of the area and was based in Guiseley, near Leeds. Established in 1877, it is now one of the oldest nursery brands in the world. It was renowned for its traditional coach built models with their suspension and wired wheels. The pram, or 'perambulator' as they were originally called, seen in this photograph, may well have been one of the latest models which incorporated the newly introduced chromium plating process of the early 1960s, which made the Silver Cross pram the envy of many a new mother.

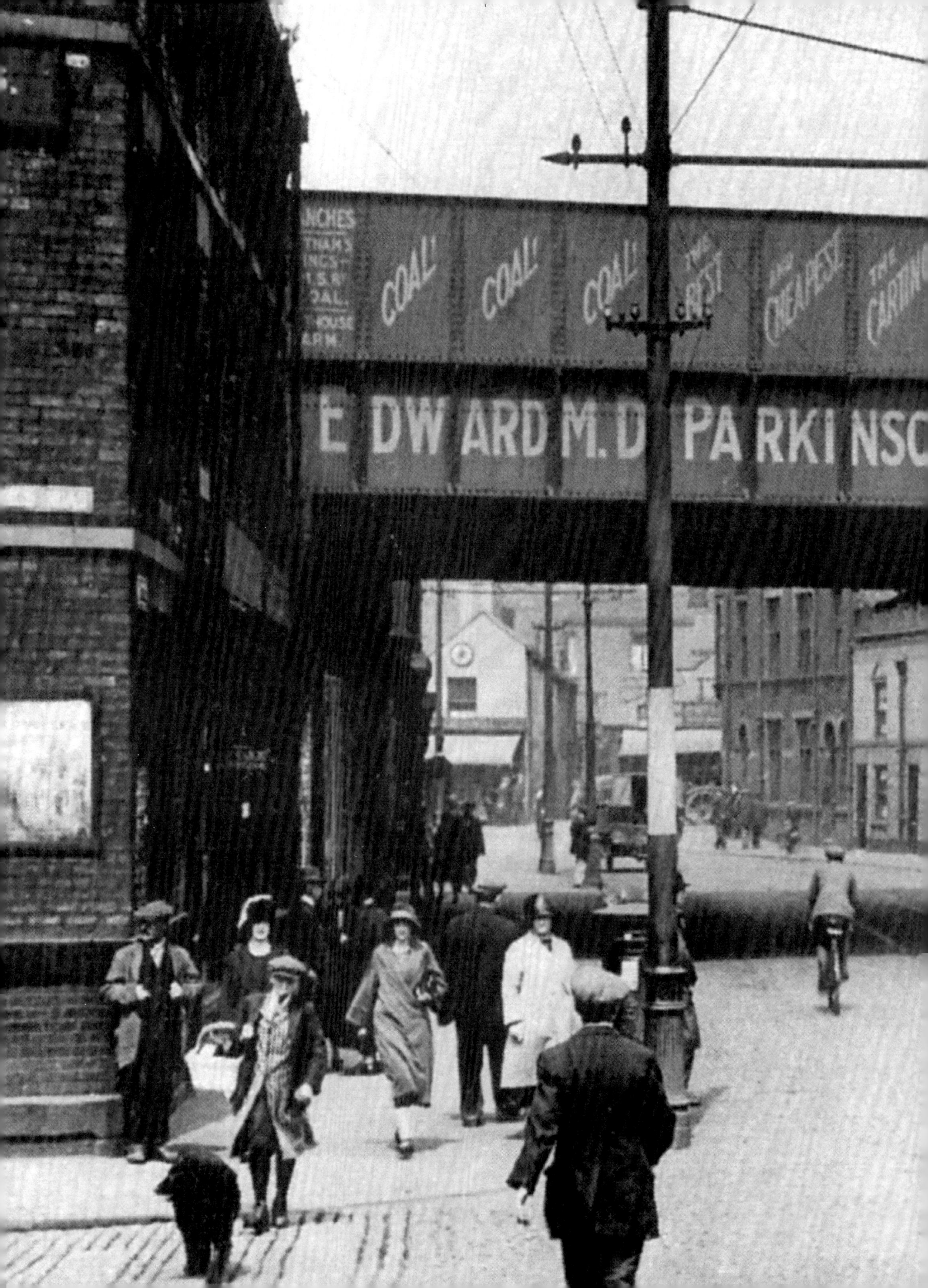
COAL!
COAL!
COAL!
THE BEST
AND CHEAPEST

TRANSPORT

This picture of a tram heading towards the bobby on point duty dates from c1920. It was on its way to Agbrigg, via Chantry Bridge, a medieval structure that replaced an original wooden one over the Calder. Advertising space is at a premium on the bridge as virtually every panel is taken up. Apart from Edward M D Parkinson, there is advertising for coal, contractors, livery stables, motors and even a funeral director. The tram was leaving behind one of our longest established pubs, on the other side of the railway bridge. Kirkgate's Grey Horse Hotel was then part of the Barnsley Brewery empire. These days, it still serves Yorkshire ales as it belongs to John Smith, the company based in Tadcaster.

Rattling along the road on the outskirts of the city, the horse-drawn bus was something of a distant cousin to those stagecoaches we had heard about in the Wild West of America. However, there were not too many Cherokees or members of the Blackfoot tribe about to make these passengers' journey a dangerous one. It was just a bumpy ride and braving the elements of the West Yorkshire weather that presented these hardy souls with any sort of problem. Pictured in 1905, this form of public transport was literally on its last legs. Electrified trams were already being seen on our roads and motorised buses would eventually become commonplace. The one pictured outside the Cathedral was a much more comfortable conveyance than its earlier counterpart. It was one of the single deckers built by the Bristol Tramways and Carriage Company, founded in 1908.

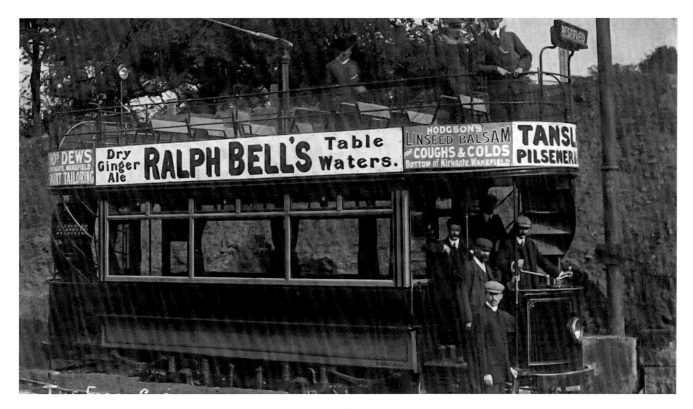

Plastered with adverts for a variety of goods and services, here is the first electric tram to be seen in Wakefield. The open topped vehicle must have given passengers a draughty perch on the upper deck and a none too comfortable ride whenever rain began to fall. The later one, shown in the accompanying photograph, has much more protection for those on board. Even so, the driver's cab was still open to the vagaries of the British climate and the man at the handle needed a warm and waterproof topcoat for much of the year. There were several lines operating in and around the Wakefield area in the early part of the last century. Electrified services were begun in the summer of 1904 by the Wakefield and District Light Railway Company as a follow-on to the horse drawn vehicles that had been running on routes used by the Omnibus Company since the 1870s. Our local trams did not serve us for very long and were consigned to history in 1932. The introduction of motor buses after the First World War accelerated their demise. Yet, they remained a nostalgic part of our heritage. It is ironic to see that they have had something of a revival in a number of towns and cities in recent years.

There is a fabulous 1920s car parked in front of the bus queue in this photograph from the Springs, almost unrecognisable in this early view. The beautiful Morris Oxford Cabriolet would have been owned by one of the more successful merchants or businessmen of the city, as cars of this type were a rarity indeed. The popular mode of transport for the majority of Wakefield people were the single decker, 20-seat buses belonging to the West Riding Automobile Company. Providing such a public service was paramount to their business and they had the foresight to have purchased a further 38 of these buses in 1924. They may have been a little uncomfortable and a little draughty but a homeward trip on one of these for a couple of pence (2d) would have been well worth it. You would have queued here for buses to far flung places like New Sharlston, Walton, Ings Cottages, Woolley and Newmillerdam. Dominent in the background of this image is Wakefield Cathedral, which was designated a Grade I listed building on 14 July, 1953. Worship began on the site of the Cathedral around Saxon times and the Normans erected parts of the first stone structure as far back as the 11th Century.

Above: There was something ironic about the word 'jams' on the side of the bus next to the statue of Queen Victoria. It was obviously part of an advert for Robertson's, Hartley's or some other fruit spread, but it could well have been the title for this photograph of the queue at the Bull Ring. Taken in the early postwar years, it shows how much we relied on public transport at that time. Car ownership was still an expensive business and only those who were, or aspiring to be, middle class could afford even a small saloon. Until better days dawned, later in the next decade, we got in line, got on board and got a ticket.

Right: It is great to see such an old photo of a majestic steam engine and Westgate Station in the background. This was Westgate in it's heyday prior to modernisation. The station was built in 1867 and the B1 Class locomotive no 61024 'Addax' is moving away from under the famous clock tower, regrettably demolished in the early 1970s. Many a happy trainspotting sortie started from here. The Thompson B1 Class were 4-6-0 steam locomotives designed for the London and North Eastern Railway by Edward Thompson for medium mixed traffic work. The first of 410 engines of the class was built in 1942. This photograph could have possibly been taken in 1962, when the Queen Mother visited West Yorkshire to attended the opening of the Delius Festival, marking the centenary of the Bradford-born composer's birth.

was acquired before the Second World War. Snapped at their new terminus, are two of Wakefield's red buses with the highly unusual centre-entrance. Previously, the Corn Exchange was the terminal point for West Riding's buses running over what was once their tram route all the way from there to Rothwell, Wakefield and Sandal. Buses serving these former tram routes had a special red and cream livery to distinguish them from the otherwise green and cream. The front vehicle was almost a veteran of the fleet, being one of five Leyland Titan buses purchased in 1936. Those boarding the AEC Regent bus on the right would do well to check both destination blinds and to consult the driver as well, who was

Above: In September 1952, Wakefield got the new bus station for which the travelling public had waited for ever since the land the deciding factor in the argument about whether the bus was on route Number 11 or 12.

WORK & INDUSTRY

Below: A crowd of onlookers gathered outside the Yorkshire Penny Bank on Westgate. They took a keen interest in the work being carried out. The labourers toiled away with purpose on a job that would benefit nearly everybody around. They were laying tram tracks for the new electrified line that would open in 1904. This modern form of travel would revolutionise public transport, making travel into and out of the city easier, quicker and so much more comfortable than ever before. Until now, people relied on horse drawn buses and carts. Shanks's pony was the only other real alternative unless you were close to a suburban railway halt.

Right: Parkinson's was founded in the early 1900s as a company dealing in horses and carriages, later becoming involved in haulage. The young lad here, Austin, son of the founder is displaying his pony and cart with pride around 1923. This transport could only have been for adverting purposes given its size, as it would never have been much use in 'continental removals' or for that matter any local ones either. Removal companies might have had all sort of slogans to attract attention, but the one chosen by Parkinson's gave the company something of a global feel to it; 'The World Moves So Do We', it's quite catchy, don't you think ?

Below: This scene has a little more substance than appears obvious at first glance; after all it is simply a local grocers in Wakefield with a lady buying her loaf of bread. But just a minute, if you can read the label on the bread you will see that it is a Warburton's Eatmore Loaf. Warburton's is the family bakers established as a small shop in the late 1800s by Thomas and his wife Ellen. Expansion of the business continued over the coming years and it continues to this day as a private, family owned business. Warburton's connection with Wakefield goes back to 1985 with the opening of a production unit which was the West End Bakery, producing loaves and bakery products for distribution throughout Yorkshire. This shopkeeper, in his white smock, would have been proud of his display and would have looked after his customers on a special one-to-one basis, as most shopkeepers of the time did. So it's a little more than a pleasant shop scene, having such a prestigious company at its heart.

ouble Two was founded as a company in Wakefield in 1940, now specialising in quality shirtmaking. It was a bold venture to launch a business at a time when manufacture of battledress and flying jackets was more the norm. Isaac Donner and Frank Myers set up their company in a small building on Kirkgate at a time when cotton was, quite simply, only available as contribution to the war effort. Consequently, the duo concentrated on manufacturing viscose shirt blouses for the women who replaced the men on the factory floor and at the assembly lines on the home front. In 1946, attention was turned to clothing the men returning to civvy street. Soft shirts with spare collar and cuffs were manufactured, and so the name of Double 2 came into being. The factory workers in this scene were at their machines in 1959. Back in 1965, socks whizzed off the machines on the factory floor. They were among the accessories that set off the fine shirts for which the company was rightly renowned.

Records suggest that the Earnshaw family has been associated with the timber trade since the late 18th century. The present fencing company was founded by Job Earnshaw in 1860. Helped by his brothers, a sawmill was established at Midgeley and work can be seen in progress in this photograph from the 1950s. In the early days, the Earnshaws made gates, fence posts, rails and parts for carts and other agricultural items. Initially, the milling was done by hand, but a steam traction engine was acquired in 1880 to modernise the works. Until the 1940s most haulage and extraction was done by horse; at one time the company owned 26 horses. The tools of the trade have changed somewhat for all long established businesses in Wakefield. The days have gone, particularly for Earnshaw's, since the company's telephone number was a simple 'Horbury 3' and the price of a 'best cart spoke' was one shilling and two pence.

William Lamb

Footwear With A Proud Heritage

William Lamb Footwear Ltd, based in Bottom Boat Road, Stanley, Wakefield, is a privately owned business that has grown since 1887 to become the United Kingdom's leading footwear distributor. It's a position the firm has achieved by being at the forefront of design, while maintaining the highest standards of production.

The company manufactures footwear for the world's largest retailers, with clients including such well known names as Walmart (Asda), Tesco, Barbour, Sainsbury's, Morrisons, John Lewis, Marks and Spencer and Next. In addition to the UK market, William Lamb shoes are also sold in the USA, Sweden, Denmark, Germany, France, Hong Kong and Japan. The company is the key footwear licensee in the UK for international brands such as Disney, Marvel, Star Wars, Peppa Pig, Thomas the Tank Engine and many others.

The business was founded in 1887 by William Lamb, the present Chairman's grandfather. William Lamb had previously been a coal miner before taking the step of setting himself up in business making the clogs then worn in the coal mines and mills of the West Riding.

Leather and wooden clog soles were made locally for many decades. When eventually larger scale manufacturing took place materials were sourced from the UK and other European countries, notably Italy. Clogs were not the only early product. During the First World War the firm produced army boots; and when the Second World War broke out production of army boots was resumed alongside the production of gas mask cases.

In 1920, in partnership with a local rhubarb grower, William Lamb also owned a cinema in Stanley (now a Gordon's car tyre depot) – inevitably it was referred to locally as 'The Clog & Rhubarb Picture House'.

Company founder William Lamb (senior) was succeeded in 1923 by his son, William Lamb (junior) - the present Chairman's father. He began to diversify production into boots as well as clogs.

In the 1950s the firm specialised in football boots, and in the 1960s in the first production of training shoes.

On William Lamb junior's death in 1966 the late Mrs Ruth Lamb became Chairman and the Joint Managing Directors were her sons David and Stuart.

In the 1960s a new fashionable footwear phenomenon began to emerge: trainers. Leisure opportunities had greatly expanded, whilst youngsters began to increasingly favour such footwear. Sales rose so high, they began to adversely impact on sales of conventional leather shoes. By 1967 William Lamb had become one of the very first UK footwear businesses to begin manufacturing what now became known simply as 'trainers', a move which proved very popular, and two further manufacturing sites were added at Ouzlewell Green and South Kirby. By the 1970s, jogging became increasingly popular, and trainers designed specifically for comfort while jogging sold well. During this manufacturing expansion in the 1970s the firm grew from employing just 35 staff to over 800 in three factories.

Today, all manufacturing is done overseas. The company's main office and large warehouse are still in Wakefield employing 85 staff, but the company also has offices in Thailand, Vietnam, China and India with a further 100 employees controlling production in those countries. The firm's strong manufacturing heritage ensures detailed control of the whole manufacturing process, from design to delivery wherever that might be in the world. The overseas business began in 1983 when Gola Sports was acquired, and importing from the Far East and Italy began.

In 2000 all the company's European manufacturing ceased.

As a business the company is committed to ensuring safe working conditions and fair treatment of employees. It takes its ethical responsibility very seriously and is proud to be recognised in the industry for its leading Ethical Trading standards.

Left and below: William Lamb clog makers and the Wm Lamb warehouse in the early days.

William Lamb Footwear is one of only three footwear members of the Ethical Trading Initiative. The ETI helps to improve working conditions for workers across the globe by setting out a code of minimum standards to be implemented into the supply chain.

Their dedicated Ethical Team consists of six people who work with their factories to improve working conditions, raise standards and meet Corrective Action Plan timescales. Four external auditors are also employed to validate the work carried out by the in-house Ethical Team.

In 2012, the company acquired the business of Rushton Ablett, in Northampton, which specialised in production of 'jellies and wellies' both in its factory in Northampton and overseas.

That same year William Lamb celebrated its 125th anniversary by presenting all employees and worldwide suppliers with commemorative matching cut glass tumblers. The company also had a Garden Party at the Lamb family's home in Walton for all employees and several suppliers also came from China, specially to attend.

Annual sales are now in excess of £55 million, a sum which in 2013 represented over eleven million pairs of shoes. Due to improvements in technology and overseas production the sale prices to the customer have remained steady whilst the volume of sales has expanded hugely.

Today, the Wakefield-based company is one of the largest footwear importers in Europe, with distribution in excess of 10 million pairs annually and a development team of 18 full-time designers. Its web-based links to its Far East offices enable rapid execution from initial concept to development samples and ultimately to bulk production.

Most categories of footwear are produced by William Lamb Footwear although there is a strong bias towards children's shoes.

Product categories in the firm's footwear portfolio include trainers, slippers, canvas, sandals, clogs, boots, wellingtons, school shoes, ladies' and men's fashion shoes, an accessories division specialising in leather goods, children's licensed bags and ladies' handbags – not least the Lamb 1887 brand founded by Charlotte Lamb.

*Top: Ruth and William Lamb. **Left:** Stuart Lamb, current Chairman of William Lamb Footwear Ltd.*

Lamb 1887
The Next Generation

I n 2010 Charlotte Lamb, Chairman Stuart Lamb's youngest daughter, founded her own handbag brand called Lamb 1887 – this was in her spare time whilst working in London as a busy corporate lawyer. This has been so successful that Charlotte has given up her day job and joined William Lamb full time to run the new handbag division as well as becoming the company's Legal Counsel. Charlotte is now the 4th generation of the family to work in the business.

Pippa Middleton and Cheryl Cole have been spotted with Lamb 1887 handbags. So have Michelle Keegan, Rosie Fortescue, Diana Vickers, Laura Whitmore and Fearne Cotton. Following the success of UK heritage brands Mulberry and Burberry, Lamb 1887 bags are tipped to become the next big thing.

Crafted from the softest leathers in classic-meets-contemporary, luxe-detail designs, the bags are as beautiful on the inside as they are on the out, each lined with luxurious suede.

Charlotte currently splits her time living between London and Yorkshire, where her studio and offices are based. "I feel lucky to be able to get the best of both worlds – although it does mean I feel like I spend my life on trains." She says: "I spent years working in the city looking for the perfect practical, super luxury, on-trend handbag that didn't break the bank, but to no avail. I decided to design and create my own range to fit into the busy working woman's lifestyle."

Her first bag was called The Ravello, a purple leather shoulder bag with a chain and leather entwined strap. "I love it because the design is very simple and chic – it really epitomised what Lamb 1887 was all about – quality materials, quality craftsmanship and simple classic design."

"The design process takes quite a long time," she says. "I gather ideas and materials over period of a few months, and then I sit down with my co-designer and we plan our collection together for the coming season."

The key factor to Lamb 1887's success, says Charlotte, lies in the classic styling, which is on-trend but also works across seasons. "We want to grow Lamb 1887 into a global brand."

Top left: Charlotte Lamb. **Below left, above and below:** A selection of beautifully crafted Lamb 1887 bags.

Woodhead Investments
Developing the Future

Woodhead Investments, now based at Woodhead House, Providence Street, Wakefield, is a family run property investment and development company, dealing with a range of retail, office, residential, industrial, and agricultural property.

Woodhead Investments and Development Services Limited, as it is known in full, was originally established as an estate agency service. Without the fortuitous meeting between Melvyn Woodhead and his future wife Susan however, one of Britain's top 1,000 private companies might never have come into existence.

Before their chance encounter, Susan was working for her father in his business which was based in Shipley. Melvyn on the other hand, was working hard to impress the estate agency, Hepper and Sons in Leeds, where he was training.
It was in 1958 that Melvyn and Susan simultaneously took a

short break from their respective jobs and both found themselves in Blackpool. It was in a hotel there that the couple first caught sight of each other. That initial glimpse was fleeting, however, as they were, at the time, passing through the hotel's revolving door! The couple soon met up again and forged a relationship which eventually led to marriage seven years later in July 1965.

Within eight weeks of marrying, the newly weds had set up their own business. In September 1965, at the age of 26 and 24 respectively, Melvyn and Susan established an estate agency service which was soon to evolve into Woodhead Investments and Development Services Limited.

*Above: Melvyn Woodhead. **Below:** The original premises in the 1960s. **Right:** M. Woodhead & Co.'s 69, Westgate End, Wakefield, premises in the 1980s.*

The couple decided upon an estate agency as their choice of business for several reasons. Melvyn was born in Wakefield and had grown up in the town. He had, therefore, an in-depth knowledge of the town and that knowledge enabled him to recognise a gap in the market and the need for an estate agency. That recognition, combined with the expertise he had built up whilst training at Hepper and Sons, and later working for the property company, Evans of Leeds, gave Melvyn a solid foundation on which to build the new business venture.

The new estate agency was initially located at 69, Westgate End, in Wakefield. Melvyn's father, George Woodhead, was a great help to the couple in their new estate agency, especially in the initial stages. George had owned several of his own small businesses during his working life, including a haulage contractors, a coal merchants and a garage. His experience, inspiration and encouragement proved of vital importance to Melvyn and Susan. Not only did George give the couple £400 to get started but he also gave them his time and indeed, after his retirement, helped out working on a part-time basis.

The estate agency set off to a flying start and soon became successful. Melvyn and Susan, aided by George, put in a lot of very hard work and dedication to build up the business. They were soon in the position to be able to hire their first employee. They took on a woman who proved to be a great help to the smooth running of the business, working part time for the firm until 1968, and paid the weekly wage of £5!

However, Melvyn's ambition did not stop there. During the time he was conducting his estate agency, he came into contact with different companies and people involved in the business. As a result, opportunities started to arise for him to actually buy properties. Melvyn's entrepreneurial spirit took over and he began to seize every positive opportunity that came his way. Indeed, almost from the very early stages of the running of the company, the property investment and development side of the business took off and was run alongside the estate agency.

The Woodheads started to buy buildings. After purchasing one the company would then refurbish and redevelop it, often turning it into apartments which would then be let to various tenants. Although the property investment and development side of the business proved to be more profitable than the original estate agency, the estate agency itself was successful in its own right.

of the business was capital intensive and less labour intensive than the estate agency. Consequently, the workforce was eventually reduced from ten to eight.

Selling the estate agency proved to be a success. The company was soon able to start renting out commercial property as well as continuing to let domestic property. Many shops and other buildings were purchased and redeveloped throughout the following years.

During the 1980s and 1990s, the company completed several major developments. As well as investing in and developing office, retail and residential space, the company also undertook many refurbishments and historical restorations. The company won Civic Award Prizes for its restoration work on the Regency Terrace - Bond Terrace, and the Georgian Terrace - St John's. In 1999, it completed Bull Ring House, a prestigious office development in the heart of Wakefield.

Left: The firm's St John's North premises in 1999. *Below:* Melvyn and Susan Woodhead in the late 1990s.

Indeed, the whole business prospered so much that only three years after its establishment new premises were needed to cope with the ever increasing business. In 1968, Melvyn and Susan moved their flourishing firm from Westgate End to the busier area of town after purchasing premises at 71 a/b Northgate for the sum of £7,500.

Being based in the busy town centre brought with it considerable advantages for the company. The estate agency gained more of a gushing river rather than a steady stream of clients. Business was booming! The increase in workload meant that extra help was needed if the estate agency was going to cope. As a result, more people were taken on and from 1973 the number staff employed rose from one to ten.

Over the following nine years both the estate agency and the property and development side of the business continued to grow. However, 1982 proved to be a ground breaking year. The Woodheads were forced to make a crucial decision about the future of their company. Running two successful similar sides of a business together began to cause more problems than it was worth, especially in regard to taxation which eventually reached a ridiculous amount. With the property and development side of the business more profitable than the estate agency, Melvyn and Susan decided that they would sell the estate agency and concentrate their efforts on property and development.

In 1982 the business changed its name to Woodhead Investments and Development Services Limited. This side

fashioned principles, keen to lend money to little and no risk clients.

In 2002 Mark and David also founded their own companies the Dreadnought Property Company Ltd and Woodhead Estates Ltd. They also have families of their own who they hope will follow in their footsteps.

Today, Woodhead Investments and Development Services Limited offers prospective clients a variety of commercial and residential property both for lease and for sale including retail, office, industrial, agricultural and car parking.

Melvyn Woodhead is affectionately known locally as 'Mr Wakefield' because of all the property his company owns in the town!

He remains responsible for overseeing the business as Chairman of Woodhead Investment, supported by sons Mark and David.

Susan, Mark and David are all actively involved in the day-to-day running of the main WIDS business, thus continuing Woodhead Services tradition as a family firm.

Mark S Woodhead, Managing Director of Woodhead Investments, focuses on the day-to-day management, refurbishment, reletting and resale of residential and commercial property. David M Woodhead BSc (Hons) MRICS, Company Secretary of Woodhead Investments, qualified as a Chartered Surveyor in 1999 and now specialises in the acquisition of residential and commercial property, rent review and lease renewal negotiations. Both, however, assist one another and can each perform each other's roles.

Although the number of official members of staff is eight, the company now employs over fifty self employed trades people on a regular basis. The Woodheads are also active members of the community and make contributions to several local charities as well as sponsoring the local St John's Middle School. Perhaps the most significant measure of the company's success, since its establishment in 1965, is its ranking in the top 1,000 of Britain's private companies in terms of asset value. Indeed, the Woodheads do not intend rest on their laurels. Already, plans to expand and diversify the portfolio have been made and no doubt the Woodhead entrepreneurial spirit will ensure that the family business continues to flourish in the future. The firm enjoys an excellent relationship with one of the world's safest banks, Handelsbanken, a Swedish bank with old

Above images: Woodhead House, one of the firm's current high quality city centre properties. **Below, from left:** Mark, Melvyn and David Woodhead, 2014.

Ridings Shopping Centre

The Heart of Shopping in Wakefield

Today, based in the heart of Wakefield, the Ridings Shopping Centre offers an exciting mix of retailers and eateries, as well as hosting regular events for all the family to enjoy. The centre is visited by millions of visitors each year.

People have been doing their shopping in Wakefield for hundreds of years, indeed, for more than a thousand years.

Wakefield has certainly been a centre of trade in England since the 1100s. A Royal Charter in 1204 gave the right to hold trading fairs in three Yorkshire cities - Wakefield, Beverley and York. The fairs in Wakefield at first offered wool, then later the wool was dyed and later still, coloured finished cloth was sold.

In Elizabethan times Wakefield held a corn market. Then, as the canal systems were developed during the 18th century and the railways during the 19th, Wakefield market sold a variety of everyday requirements. In 1847 Wakefield Borough Market Company was formed which put up a market hall. People shopped in the area bounded by Westgate, the Bull Ring and the Cathedral and stalls began to develop into shops along the narrow streets that made up Cross Square.

The Market Cross was the focus until it was removed in 1866.

*Left: The old Market Cross. **Below and above right:** Construction of the Ridings Shopping Centre in 1981.*

In late 1978 an outline plan was submitted for a covered shopping centre, some extension of existing shops and 850 new parking spaces. All relevant bodies were consulted to make sure no safety or building regulations would be broken and that no-one's right would be abused.

Progress was rapid, and by April of the following year all necessary permission had been granted for the outline plan and a road closure order was drafted. This was necessary as a new road network was planned to make the new centre easily accessible. The drafted order was confirmed by the Secretary of State in March 1980.

Now the developers, Capital & Counties, could firm up their ideas and more detailed plans were submitted. Two groups of officials guided the project through a minefield of laws and regulations. A control group dealt with matters of principle and a steering group dealt with their application in the detailed tasks that had to be done.

For some years in the 20th century trade flourished, but after the Second World War other towns began to take precedence over Wakefield for shopping in Yorkshire. In an attempt to put things right for Wakefield the market was rebuilt in 1964. Soon, new streets were built, including Brook Street, Teall Street and Westmoreland Street. Two years later a major shopping and housing development was proposed. It was built between 1968 and 1971 and included the shops between the Kirkgate precinct and George Street, the Almshouse Lane multi-storey car park and four blocks of flats.

Left: A poster announcing the opening of the 'The Ridings'. Below: A view inside The Ridings from the mid-1990s.

In 1974, the Wakefield Metropolitan District Council, formed by the reorganisation of local government, produced another scheme of improvements. This time the aim was to create the Cathedral precinct with pedestrian areas, landscaping round the immediate area of the Cathedral, and the provision of facilities for the disabled. Those changes were finished in 1977, just in time for the Queen's visit to Wakefield in her Silver Jubilee year.

Competition from other towns and cities, however, still meant a loss of trade in Wakefield. These developments hit Wakefield particularly hard because a high percentage of its shopping trade had been in food and domestic convenience goods. The council had to find some way of bringing the sale of durable goods, those items such as clothes and furniture that are bought less often, into Wakefield's city centre. Shops that had managed to remain open in the city were having trouble expanding and improving their services because of limited site ownership.

At the same time, land alongside these shops was under-used. It was decided to take 6.6 acres, then the site of a dance hall, a car park and so on, and turn them into a modern, attractive and convenient shopping mall.

The Centre was built to a unique design, so that shoppers could enter and exit from the street on all levels. Peter Spawforth, who was the chief planning officer at the Council at the time, had travelled to America and Canada in search of ideas.

As a result The Ridings was revolutionary, boasting the first Food Court in the UK and the first glass wall climber lift.

The site originally housed a number of older buildings: two doctors' surgeries, the Salvation Army, a pub, a dance hall, a car park, public toilets, baths and roads. All the existing occupiers were either re-housed on or off site, or otherwise compensated.

A quarry was discovered in the early stage of building. It is thought to date back to when stone was cut for the Cathedral construction. The lower mall, which originally opened in 1972 and traded as an open shopping precinct, was incorporated into the new scheme with a new glazed roof and updated finishes and services to meet the standards of the rest of the Centre.

To pick up ideas from people who had experience in setting up similar schemes, the Wakefield Metropolitan District Council and Capital & Counties jointly paid for a study tour of shopping centres in New York, Boston, Atlanta and Toronto.

Some 2.5 million people live within a 30 minute drive of The Ridings, resulting in some 200,000 visits each week, over 10.5 million visitors a year

At the time of its opening on 17 October, 1983, The Ridings was architecturally and economically the most innovative development in the region. It was one of the UK's forerunners in the development of the American concept of covered shopping malls with integrated customer facilities.

Work began on the Ridings centre early in 1981 and took 2 1⁄2 years, and £23 million to complete. Located at the rear of existing shops on Kirkgate and Little Westgate (opposite the Cathedral), the external brickwork was designed in such a way that the centre blends into the established Wakefield townscape, nestling comfortably among surrounding buildings.

More than 4,000 people walked through the doors on the Sunday before the official opening, even though it was before Sunday trading hours were introduced and they couldn't buy anything. Excited children from across the district were given a half day off when The Ridings officially opened on Monday 17 October so that they could visit the pioneering centre.

Over 1,200 people worked at the Centre when it first opened, in addition to over 40 people employed directly by the Ridings Centre Management as well as numerous contract staff.

This page: *Exterior and interior views of The Ridings Centre, the place for fantastic value shopping with over 80 stores offering a great mix of big brand names and unique independent stores all under cover.*

Originally developed by Capital & Counties in partnership with Wakefield Metropolitan District Council and designed by architects, Chapman Taylor Partners, The Ridings was named after the three historic divisions of Yorkshire, the North, West and East Ridings.

In 2008 £2.5 million was spent refurbishing the Centre, this involved new entrances for Cathedral Walk, Almshouse and Kirkgate, new lifts with glass and natural light was used to enhance the Centre.

Today, The Ridings houses more than 85 stores and a selection of cafes and eateries with over 1,000 car parking spaces. The Ridings employs 40 members of staff, three of whom joined the Centre when it first opened its doors.

Offering a selection of big name brands and independent retailers, some such as BHS, Boots, Marks and Spencer and Morrisons have been in The Ridings since it first opened. The Centre continues to attract new tenants and renewals.

Complementing existing retailers, The Ridings also hosts a number of 'pop-up' boutiques and fairs, a monthly craft market and there are also a growing number of co-operative run stores. A full schedule of family friendly and exciting events has also helped keep footfall high.

Barbara Winston, Centre Manager, says: "The Ridings has celebrated some fantastic achievements since its opening and we're delighted that shoppers, both new and old, keep returning. There have been many changes to the retail landscape over the last three decades, but by listening to our customers and retailers and by constantly being innovative, The Ridings remains an immensely popular and much loved attraction."

Above: A poster celebrating 30 years serving generations of Wakefield and beyond. *Below:* Crowds flock to The Ridings vintage fair in 2013.

ESSECO UK LIMITED
Continuing the Legacy of Lord Brotherton

Esseco UK Limited is the current incarnation of a company that was founded in 1878 as Dyson Sons and Brotherton.

Its founder, Edward Brotherton, the eldest of six children from a Manchester family involved in the textile trade, was born in 1856. In 1878, at the age of just 22, he realised that many chemical manufacturers were pouring away a fortune in ammonia by-products. He approached the Dysons of Middlesbrough and they agreed to back him to the tune of £3,000 to form a new chemical company in Wakefield.

During this time Edward lived in a small cottage in the middle of the Wakefield site and it soon became surrounded by more and more chemical plants as the business expanded.

From its earliest beginnings the Company specialised in the manufacture of ammonia salts. Over the years the Company broadened the product range, but always maintained a key position in ammonia salts.

1881 was a busy year for Edward. He expanded onto another site at Holme Street in Leeds, adjacent to the City's gas works, so that ammonia liquor could be pumped from the works to the Wakefield site for processing. Edward bought out the Dysons and the Company became known as Brotherton & Co. He also opened a central office in Park Row, Leeds.

In 1882, on the eve of his marriage to Mary Jane Brookes, Edward moved out of his cottage on the Wakefield site, but sadly a year later his young wife died in childbirth along with their baby. During the months following his wife's death Edward devoted his time to expanding his business. He never married again, choosing instead to lavish his affections on his nephews and nieces.

Edward continued to grow the business and by 1884 had secured a 5 year contract with the Halifax gas works to process their ammonia liquors.

His success continued and in 1888 he acquired another site at Stourton, where he established a tar distillation operation which complimented the activities at the Leeds and Wakefield sites.

Further expansion followed over the next decade in Birmingham, Glasgow, Leeds, Liverpool, Middlesbrough, Sunderland, Wakefield and Workington, building on Edward's knowledge and experience in efficiently handling ammonia liquors.

Expansion of the Wakefield site continued and production of new products such as ammonium carbonate commenced, resulting in a forest of tall chimneys and towers which dominated the Wakefield skyline. Ammonium carbonate is still manufactured on the Wakefield site today.

As well as continuing a successful business empire, Edward entered parliament in the election of 1902, with the slogan "A Wakefield man for Wakefield".

On June 23rd 1902, three days before the coronation of King Edward VII, every child on the register of any public elementary school in Wakefield received a "Coronation Pass Book" with a deposit of one shilling from Edward Brotherton to celebrate the event and to encourage saving and thrift amongst children. It came with a letter with the following items of advice "Take care of the pence; the pounds will look after themselves. A penny wasted is a penny gone forever. A penny saved is a penny gained. Remember money makes money."

Top, facing page: Founder, Edward Allen Brotherton. Bottom, facing page: A 1940s Thorneycroft Brotherton lorry. Above: Edward (front row, 8th from the left) and his employees, September 1921. Below: The Calder Vale Road factory ca. 1940.

In 1904, Edward's eldest nephew, Charles Ratcliffe, joined the Company and took his uncle's name. In the same year Edward created the Brotherton Charity Trust for pensioners, 5 years before any state pension scheme existed.

By 1905, Edward's business had grown to such an extent that he was warmly referred to as the "Ammonia King of England" and he moved his headquarters to the City Chambers in Leeds.

Buoyed by his business success, Edward repeated his act of generosity to the children of Wakefield in celebration of his 50th birthday. He was also re-elected for a second term as MP for Wakefield.

In the years leading up to the First World War, Brotherton & Co. went from strength to strength reflecting the increasing prosperity of the country. At the outbreak of war Edward raised and equipped the 15th Battalion of the West Yorkshire Regiment, known as the "Leeds Pals", gaining him the rank of Honorary Colonel. Brotherton & Co. supported the war effort by producing essential materials across a number of the manufacturing sites. He lent the British Treasury £500,000 for the War Loan Fund, giving all of the interest earned to the Exchequer.

After the First World War, Edward served another term as an MP. He also had a special medal designed and presented it, along with a small amount of money, to soldiers who had suffered as prisoners of war. His generosity continued with donations to various organisations, including: Toc H (a soldiers' rest and recreation centre established during the war), the YMCA, the Salvation Army, Wakefield Hospital and the Marie Curie Radium Fund, as well as various church funds, parish and village halls, public parks and devastated regions of France.

In 1921, Edward became chairman of the Leeds University advisory committee of the Department of Pathology and Bacteriology, and donated £20,000 "to be devoted to the development of bacteriological study and research in the interests of public health".

Today the Company still operates in Wakefield from the original Calder Vale Road site as Esseco UK Ltd and is a major supplier of chemicals to both the domestic and international markets.

The current product range remains focused on ammonia salts, but the product portfolio began expanding from 2006 onwards. This led to a significant investment by Esseco in 2010, including a new sulphur burning plant which produces a range of bisulphite products for use in a number of industries from food and beverage to oil extraction. The Company also specialises in the production of aviation runway de-icers and over the past 3 years has invested in new plants and equipment to support this activity. The remainder of the chemical production involves the use of other key raw materials including sulphur dioxide, carbon dioxide, alkali hydroxides and several organic acids.

In 1927, Edward donated £100,000 towards the cost of new library buildings for Leeds University. Edward was given the honour of laying the first stone in 1929 and donated a further £30,000 for maintenance and administration of the library.

In 1928, to mark the Company's Golden Jubilee, Edward gave each of his workers a gold sovereign for each year of service.

In 1929, Edward was elevated to the Peerage and turned to his adopted city for his title, becoming Lord Brotherton of Wakefield.

Lord Brotherton died in 1930 after a long illness. He bequeathed a second donation of £100,000 towards the new library at Leeds University. The library was opened in his name on October 6th 1936. It houses his personal collection of historic books and manuscripts which he pledged before his death.

Edward Brotherton left an inspiring legacy and is quoted as having said "Unsparing effort is the whole secret of success in industry and business".

In the years after Edward's death the Company changed hands several times. It has been owned by Albright & Wilson Ltd, E Green & Son Ltd, who remain present in Wakefield today but have no business links to the current Company, the US multinational Church and Dwight Co., Inc. of Arm and Hammer™ Toothpaste fame and more latterly, since 2008, by the Italian company Esseco Group Srl.

Investment at the Wakefield site continues with a new manufacturing plant, designed to produce an agricultural fertiliser, currently under construction and due for completion by the end of 2014.

If Lord Brotherton were alive today, he would be rightly proud of what his first chemical company has achieved over the last 136 years and the current Company is sure that he would be supportive of the plans for the rest of the 21st Century.

Top, facing page: The Calder Vale Road factory today, 2014.
Bottom, facing page: The Calder Vale Road offices in 2012.
Above: Sulphur burner plant built in 2010. Below: 2 x 1000 tonne de-icer stock tanks (left) and the new ATS plant under construction, 2014.

YPO

Delivering better value for the public sector

Y PO, based at 41 Industrial Park, Wakefield, is the largest public sector buying organisation in the UK. The business is 100% publicly owned; all profits are reinvested in the public sector – with a total of £105 million returned to date.

The organisation marked its Ruby Anniversary in 2014.

Tracing its roots back to 1915, YPO began life at Heath Common as West Riding County Supplies. Later moving to Cliff Lane, the enterprise was reborn in 1974 as the Yorkshire Purchasing Organisation. The original members were West Yorkshire County Council, North Yorkshire County Council, Barnsley, Rotherham, Bradford, Calderdale, Doncaster, Kirklees and Wakefield.

In 1974, the workforce comprised 185 warehouse staff and 147 office staff. They concentrated on delivering items to schools and local government establishments;

goods were held in the warehouse at Balne Lane. These included food and text books. Larger items, including furniture, could be delivered to the customer straight from the supplier. An Essential Clothing section at Balne Lane and several outlets across Yorkshire supplied school clothing. The customer base grew from 6,000 in April 1974 to over 8,000 by November of that year.

In addition, the organisation was making contractual arrangements which allowed customers to order goods and services directly from manufacturers. In fact, this was seen as the main area for expansion with heating fuels, building materials and transport requirements playing a big part. When the first annual accounts were published in 1975, a total £14m turnover was reported.

In 1980, Cliff Lane closed down and all the office staff moved to a new headquarters at Park Lodge Lane, in Wakefield. In the early 1980s, the Food section of the business was re-located to its present warehouse at Flanshaw. In 1985, a new warehouse opened at 41 Industrial Estate. Office-based staff re-located there in 1993.

Today, the organisation is known simply as YPO following a rebrand in 2012.

Top left: YPO's former head quarters at Park Lodge Lane.
Centre and below: Old and modern YPO catalogues.

In April 2014, the full board and senior management were in attendance at the 40th anniversary celebrations. They particularly acknowledged three members of staff who had been with the organisation for the full 40 years; Christine Preston, Alan Roe and John Goldthorpe.

Christine Preston said: "YPO is a fantastic place to work. Times have certainly changed over the years. When I first started in 1974, all orders were processed manually and we took calls with just two phones! I've seen people come and go,

electricity to power one million street lights, and more than 1.25 million hours of temporary labour.

How times have changed. A flick through the 1974 catalogue gives a good indication of those changes. Items available to buy that year included ink wells and ink well fillers, sealing wax, typewriter ribbons, carbon paper – and most surprisingly petticoats.

Today, with over 500 employees, and offering a range of 27,000 products and 100 service contracts, YPO continues to be a leader in its field. In 2014, YPO won Supplier of the Year at the Education Resources Awards, and Best Public Procurement Project at the CIPS Supply Management Awards alongside partner procurement organisations.

YPO continues to be focused on growth, with a strategy to improve online ordering after the successful launch of a new e-commerce website in February 2014. In September, the YPO member authorities also established a new limited company, enabling YPO to trade with new markets and bringing even more growth to the organisation.

Left: Opening of the new offices at 41 Industrial Park in 1993. Above: A YPO delivery vehicle. Below: Celebrating 40 years in business.

and sometimes come back again! It's been my only job since leaving school; it's been a pleasure to come to work every day and I've met some great people along the way. I haven't regretted a single moment."

Simon Hill, Managing Director of YPO said: "YPO employees through the decades have worked tirelessly to help our public sector customers make best use of their ever squeezed budgets, whether it's schools, local authorities, charities, the NHS or the emergency services. They are a talented and highly skilled group and we wanted to applaud their achievements. They have helped us go from strength to strength as an organisation."

Each year YPO sells: more than 1.5 million eggs, 140 million Post-It Notes, 30 million exercise books, 230 tons of glue sticks, 5 million pom-poms, enough

ACKNOWLEDGMENTS

The publishers would like to sincerely thank the following individuals and organisations for their help and contribution to this publication.

Mirrorpix

dusashenka's photostream - www.flickr.com/photos/oldcinemaphotos/

Yorkshire Weekly Newspaper Group Ltd

Wakefield Museum

Wakefield Learning and Local Studies Library

Ossett Library